FOOTPRINTS IN COURAGE

Kristin Gilpatrick

Badger Books Inc.
Oregon, WI

© Copyright 2002 by Kristin Gilpatrick Halverson
Published by Badger Books Inc.
Cover design by Ann Christianson
Edited by Julie Shirley
All photos courtesy of Alf Larson unless otherwise indicated
Printed by McNaughton & Gunn of Saline, Mich.

First edition

ISBN 1-878569-90-2

Badger Books Inc.
P.O. 192, Oregon, WI 53575
Toll-free phone: (800) 928-2372
Web site: http://www.badgerbooks.com
E-Mail: books@badgerbooks.com

To the defenders of Bataan and Corregidor, whose valiant service to the cause of freedom was repaid with a suffering that defied human imagination. And, to all former prisoners of war and combat soldiers who know what it is to walk a mile in such anguished footsteps. Each one of you has earned America's eternal gratitude.

CONTENTS

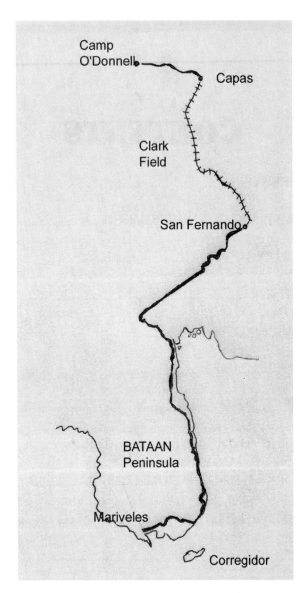

The route of the Bataan Death March.

FOREWORD

The surrender of the Philippine Peninsula of Bataan, the horrifying aftermath that followed in the Bataan Death March and the torturous imprisonment of thousands of Allied servicemen is a little known and largely forgotten tragedy of World War II.

The American military stations guarding the Philippines in peacetime were unprepared for the island nation's invasion by the Japanese, which began Dec. 8, 1941. The pending war in Europe was the priority for shipments of war material from the United States, and so the Philippine defense armaments and air support were mostly World War I grade.

In addition, the island's codefenders, the Filipino army, was largely untrained and ill equipped. When the superior Japanese forces broke through the Filipino front lines in a few days, the Imperial Army captured the defenders' stockpile of supplies. As a result, the remaining defense of the Philippines was fought with inadequate food and medical provisions. Large numbers of soldiers were sick and starving as the American and Filipino armies tried valiantly to push the Japanese back, and then to just keep them from penetrating farther. In a few weeks time, the men and women of Bataan found themselves virtually cut off from the world and all hope of reinforcements.

Starving and running low on everything but pure defiance, Major Gen. Edward P. King surrendered the

10,000 American and 65,000 Filipino defenders April 9, 1942.

Some 1,000 Americans and 10,000 Filipinos would not survive the next 10 days, as the Japanese subjected their prisoners to an ordeal that today's historians call The Bataan Death March and survivors still call "The Hike."

On April 12, 1942, the Japanese gathered the surrendered men, formed them into columns and began marching the prisoners in groups of 100 toward an ill-prepared concentration camp, some 80 hot and hard miles away.

The marchers were given virtually no food or water and forced at bayonet point to march onward in the sweltering heat. Those who succumbed to thirst, heat, illness, or exhaustion, were beheaded, shot, tortured, trampled or even buried alive in front of their fellow marchers.

Those who willed themselves to keep walking were "rewarded" with nearly four more years of subhuman existence. These prisoners survived each day for years on rice and water. They lived one day, one hour, one minute at a time, enduring endless days of forced labor, starvation, physical and psychological torture, deprivation, boredom, and bizarre, painful, and untreated illnesses.

One of the American prisoners wrestling his conditions and his own mind to survive was Alf Larson of Crystal, Minnesota.

Larson's story of World War II combat in the Philippines and his subsequent years in captivity as a prisoner of war is a tale so powerful and horrific that he pushed it into the recesses of his memory for 55 years.

Then, at age 81, Larson met Rick Peterson, a man who would share his history with the future. The two met while Larson was volunteering at the Minnesota

Zoo, where Peterson was working. Peterson had studied World War II and the Holocaust of Jews in Germany for more than 40 years and had long hoped to write a story of survival from this period in history.

Like so many war veterans, Larson rarely spoke of his experiences to anyone, including his wife and children. A few years after Larson and Peterson met, the former prisoner of war agreed to tell his new friend his story. Reliving the horror of it all in detail was no easy task, however. The months of recorded interviews, begun in 1999, stirred up nightmares Larson had long forgotten.

As Peterson painstakingly transcribed the interviews and traveled twice to the Philippines to retrace Larson's anguished footsteps (see Epilogue), he gained new, often disturbing, and even inspiring insights into the prisoner of war experience, the endurance of the human body, and the strength of the human spirit. Peterson soon believed that Larson's story would be best served if it was shared with other Americans who had long forgotten, or never knew of, the sacrifices of the soldiers on Bataan.

Peterson began by posting his transcription on a Web site designed by Jake Carlson and telling his story through local media.

A mutual friend, Bill von Bank, introduced me to Peterson's work and Larson's incredible human testament in 2001. Peterson was eager to share Larson's story and asked for my help in transforming his transcripts and research into a book.

As a war history author and founder of Operation Freedom Appreciation*, I had long wanted to write about the forgotten battles of World War II.

In the past five years, as I've spoken about World War II in classrooms and community halls, I've often noted how little people know about the war that raged in the Pacific between Pearl Harbor and the dropping of the atomic bomb on Hiroshima. I've discovered that Americans know less about the fall and rise of the Philippines during World War II, especially about the men and women who survived that fall and its chilling aftermath. That aftermath, the story of the surrender, the Bataan Death March, and Japanese imprisonment defies human imagination and dignity. The Bataan survival story is one of the most horrific tales of cruelty and unfathomable courage to come out of World War II.

I wholeheartedly agreed with Peterson that Alf Larson's experiences as a Death March survivor were a piece of history that should be saved for the next generation of Americans to study, learn and gain inspiration from. I am honored to share a part in that noble endeavor.

As I interviewed Larson, researched the POW experience, and transformed Larson's memories into book form, I was often deeply saddened, sickened, angry, and most of all, inspired by his and others' Death March and prisoner of war survival stories.

At its simplest, what follows is one man's story of survival against horrific odds. Yet it is my hope that the events captured on these pages will stand as a printed memorial to the thousands of heroes like Alf Larson who gave their last full measure in defense of Bataan, in protection of their friends, in the fight for their own survival, and in service to a grateful nation.

* To find out how to participate in Operation Freedom Appreciation, visit www.heronextdoor.org/freedom.html

FOOTPRINTS IN COURAGE

TRAVELING TO THE 'PROMISED LAND'

Alf Larson in 1939.

Alf Larson's story begins as it ends, with a long journey home.

Born July 29, 1918, in Orebro, Sweden, Larson was just four years old when he took his first trip abroad. He traveled to the United States as an immigrant with his parents, brother Gust and sister Anna at the invitation of a cousin in Duluth, Minnesota, who promised "streets paved with gold" upon their arrival.

Larson's father, Gutav, booked his family steerage accommodations on the Gripsholm sailing ship for a September 1922 arrival at Ellis Island, New York.

Though Larson's first long trip was exciting, it was not easy.

"We were on the third level down, which is in the forward end at the very bottom of the ship. We had one room with bunks for our entire family and used a common bathroom in the hallway. At one point, some yokel left a porthole open and part of the inside deck was flooded. Everything got wet in our section but there was no damage.

"Then, we ran into a storm coming over so the passage was kind of rough, and I was the only one in our family who wasn't seasick."

Upon their arrival in Duluth, the family found no golden streets and only hard times, at least at first. "We had rented in a rough part of town, and it was so cold inside that during the night the water would freeze. We moved out of there as quickly as possible. My father had been a chief electrical inspector in Sweden, which was a good white-collar job. Initially, the only job he could get was packing fish, though he did eventually get back into electrical engineering."

Despite the hardships, the family proved survivors and hung on even during The Great Depression when food and other supplies were hard to come by.

"The only meat we had was what I could poach (illegally hunt), and I was good at hunting. Game Warden Koppi was always saying, 'I'm going to get you one of these days,' but he was a nice guy and never really tried too hard, and I was able to put some meat on the table."

When Larson graduated from Morgan Park High School in 1937, jobs were still scarce, so he joined his electrical engineer brother in Baton Rouge, Louisiana, where Larson grew "sicker than a dog" from working around the toxic chemicals at the plant. After six months, Larson returned to Duluth to find a new job. He joined the Army's Civilian Conservation Corps in Brimson, Minnesota, and spent six months mapping much of northeast Minnesota before he was discharged in March 1939.

Unable to find work, Larson took his CCC lieutenant's advice and joined the Army, enlisting at Fort Snelling, Minnesota, for a three-year stint in the U.S. Army Air Corps, he said, "without the smallest idea of what I was getting into!"

Following basic and infantry training at Fort Snelling, the recruits were trucked to Camp McCoy, Wisconsin, for two weeks of infantry training.

It was on the return journey that Larson's got his first taste of the rigors of long marches when the recruits marched back to Fort Snelling, some 150 miles, and about 85 miles farther than Larson would hike in the infamous Bataan Death March.

This time, though, Larson was hiking under much better conditions.

"We would march twenty miles each day with a few rest stops and a break for lunch, then march until about 6 p.m. when we would stop for the night and set up camp, which consisted of setting up our pup tents (each man had one-half of a pup tent so we had to have a partner to set up the tent). After camp was set, we had supper (our mess hall kitchen followed us the entire march). We were roused up at about 5 a.m., had breakfast, broke camp and repeated the scenario all over again. We marched in full battle gear, that is, rifle, ammunition, gear and all (about seventy to eighty pounds).

"On the last night before reaching Minneapolis, we marched our twenty miles, set up camp for the night

Alf Larson stands in front of a native Philippine hut before the war.

and then, about 9 p.m., we were awakened and told we would have a forced march lasting all night to reach Minneapolis to simulate battle conditions. We were a really tired bunch when we reached Fort Snelling. Everybody not scheduled for some kind of duty was given a three-day pass. I used mine to catch a Greyhound bus home to Duluth."

Still foot-sore but eager for more adventure than infantry training had to offer, Larson opted for duty in a new "promised land," the jungle paradise of the Philippines. Though he knew better to believe the jungle was "paved in gold," the idea of being stationed on a warm, exotic beach seemed like a good one.

"Two infantry guys kept bugging me to go to the Philippines, saying 'it's wonderful duty over there.' So, when we got back to Fort Snelling, I applied for and received a transfer to the U.S. Army Air Corps in the

Philippines Islands. I later found out those two guys had been there, didn't like it, and 'bought out.'"

But by then, Larson's fate had been sealed. He applied for and received his transfer to the Army Air Corps in the Philippines and shipped out in October 1939. He traveled by train to San Francisco's Angel Island overseas replacement base and stayed one last week on U.S. soil before boarding an old World War I German tanker, the U.S.S. Grant, in the San Francisco harbor.

As the ship pulled past the Golden Gate Bridge, Larson had no idea how far from home he'd be, nor for how long. Unbeknownst to him, the Minnesota native was embarking on a six-year journey.

The long voyage once again proved less than ideal as storms rocked the ship on its way to Hawaii. "Some guys got sick and lost their cookies all over everything, but again I didn't get seasick. It wasn't that uncomfortable a journey for me. We were bunked in a room with nine to twelve bunks in it, had movies shown each night and two good meals a day."

Any discomfort was quickly forgotten anyway when the ship docked in Oahu, Hawaii, for a one-day layover. "We got to go ashore and they had a hula gal's show for us, free of charge. When I got up to leave, the others had already gone, and I didn't know where the heck they went. I went through an exit and ended up, embarrassingly, in the ladies dressing room!"

The island company was much more subdued at the ship's next day stop in Guam where Larson saw only some local residents in a small village.

Any excitement Larson had for his final Philippine destination quickly evaporated in the tropical island heat the day the ship docked for good in late October 1939. "A big typhoon had come, and that first day it was so hot and humid, much hotter than Louisiana had ever been. It was a fitting welcome! I thought, 'This is lower than Lower Slobovia! What the heck have I got into here?'"

With no way to imagine what the heat would be like during the next five years in the Philippines (and one more in Japan), the 22-year-old went to his duty station as an air corps mechanic and crew chief.

Larson soon realized that, though the tropics were not the paradise he dreamed of, the Filipino people were good company.

"Because the Philippines had been a possession of America for years, many of them could speak some English. One time, we went to one island, Mindora, south of Luzon. A delegation from town came and met us and invited us to join them in a wedding celebration they were having. We didn't know anybody, but they treated us like kings! We stayed overnight in tents and some time during the night, a twelve-foot python came crawling through the campsite. We tried to tell this knucklehead with us to leave it alone and let it just slither away, but he went and shot him with a 30-caliber rifle! Well, that snake thrashed around and tore our tent and stuff to pieces. That snake caused a heck of a lot of damage before he died."

In addition to the friendly locals he met, Larson was pleasantly surprised by how easily he seemed to acclimate to the stifling heat.

"I think that's because I didn't do what the medics suggested. We worked from 8 a.m. to noon when everything—and I mean everything—got locked up because the medics said we should take a nap after lunch when the day was its hottest. I tried that but I got so doggone lazy I didn't want to get out of bed, so I said 'to heck with this!' I bought a bicycle and hit the countryside while everyone slept. I pedaled all around southern Luzon — anyplace there was a road. One time I biked from Nichols Field to Cavite, which is about twenty-five miles from Manila. I ate with the Marines and came back the same day.

"I believe all that pedaling acclimated me to the heat faster, got me in great physical shape, and made me able to endure the Philippines — and maybe even the Death March — better than some. The fact that I was healthy and very fit prior to the war and the march helped me endure it. The guys that were real partiers and carousers before the war generally didn't survive the captivity."

Larson gradually worked his way up from airplane mechanic to crew chief and eventually flight engineer stationed with the aircraft supply and maintenance group, the 27th Material Squadron, at Nichols Field outside Manila. "As a flight engineer, my duty was to ensure the aircraft was kept in tip top flying condition."

Larson was one of 5,000 to 6,000 working in a combination bombardment and pursuit group, with the B-10 as the standard bomber and P-26 as the standard fighter. There, an old World War I gunner named "Pop" took Larson under his wing and taught him the airmen ropes — ropes he first learned as flight engineer riding on an A09 Grumman Amphibious Observation airplane.

At first Larson flew on the A09 about four hours a

month with Nichols Field commander Colonel Ryan, who claimed the bird as his own, at least until the higher-ranking Colonel George (the aviation liaison in the Philippines) wanted the plane. "While Colonel Ryan had control of the air-

Alf Larson rides around the Philippines in pre-war days.

plane, we only flew four hours per month, just long enough for the colonel to draw his flight pay, so a lot of my time was spent polishing the airplane and sitting around. That changed when Colonel George claimed the AO9. He flew the pants off us! We were hardly ever at Nichols Field after that and visited every place we had an auxiliary field because he wanted to go to all the bases in the Philippines and check the facilities and supplies."

Larson got in good with Colonel George nearly from the start. "One time on the way to Delmonte, the engine ran away, meaning the prop went wild. Well, I worked all night and got it running again by morning. That got me in good with him."

"Soon after, the colonel inquired about my flight engineer's pay scale, and within two days, I received orders that said my per diem pay was to be exactly the same as the officers. So every time we left base, I got $6 too, and we continued to fly all over the islands."

Larson's flights took on more serious tones in November 1941, when the unit began flying combat observation missions with the understanding that they were to engage any enemy (Japanese) aircraft they saw. Even though America was not yet at war with Japan, American military stations were put on a war alert in November 1941, and Japanese aircraft — which were often seen flying reconnaissance missions over the Philippines — were considered enemy aircraft.

In addition, Larson's long-awaited orders to ship home were frozen. He was due to be discharged from the service in October 1941 but, like many of the men trapped during the looming Japanese invasion of the Philippines, Larson's dreams of returning to civilian life would have to wait many more years.

Given the war alert, Larson added his battle station duty as a B-10 gunner to his flight engineer duties on the AO9. The air crews also practiced engaging the enemy.

"When I flew on combat patrols, I flew as the top turret gunner. Our guns were loaded but you couldn't fire on the way out unless you saw enemy aircraft. On the way in, you could expend the ammunition, and we would empty the guns by shooting at porpoise or stingray down in the water. For gunnery practice, we also had aircraft that would tow targets we would shoot at. We got pretty good with the machine guns. When we hit the target latch, the tail would fall to the ground. Then, the ground crew would have to go and pick up a new one, so they got mad at us when we hit the targets — man, they were mad at us!"

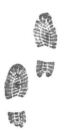

HOLDING ON

For Americans, World War II started when the Japanese attacked Pearl Harbor, Hawaii, December 7, 1941.

"That was December 8 at our end of the world," says Larson, who learned of the Japanese attack from a mess sergeant.

"Prior to this we had had incidents where Japanese had penetrated our airspace but still, even when we got the word about the Japs' attack, we didn't believe it."

Their naiveté wore off in a hurry.

That same day, Larson was on a crew ordered to fly photographic equipment from Nichols Field up to bombers at Clark Field who were preparing to photograph strategic positions on Formosa.

"We got on board the A09 and for armament I had a 45-caliber submachine gun (a Tommy Gun) and the other crewmembers had 45-caliber pistols. We were now at war with the Japanese and that was all our armament! We took the doors off the plane so we could see outside but luckily didn't see any Japanese before we landed at Clark Field."

It would be the last time in the next four years that Larson could look around and report no Japanese. At about 1245 some 50 Japanese fighters and 50-plus bombers attacked Clark Field.

"Our officers left to deliver the photo material and I

Filipinos work in a rice paddy shortly before the peaceful field became a battleground.

was sitting by the plane when somebody said, "Gee, look at how the Navy is flying up there. Look at that formation." Well, I took one look and shouted, "It's Japs!"

The Clark Field commandant had made his troops dig trenches, and I dove into one when the Japs started strafing the field. Shortly after that, bombs came whistling down like you wouldn't believe. They plastered us for about one-half hour. Then their fighters came and strafed us again. I was shooting at them with my 45-caliber submachine gun. I don't know if I hit anything, but it sure made me feel good to shoot back!"

Larson survived his first moments in combat unscathed, but the Clark Field pursuit base was not so lucky. The Japanese had obliterated their target, destroying the A09 Larson got there in, nearly all the B-17 bombers and most of the P-40 fighters. By now, the U.S. forces in the Far East had fewer than twenty bombers and forty fighters to defend themselves with, a number that continued to shrink rapidly.

The air raid damaged more than just equipment, however. Several airmen around Larson were wounded or worse in the attack.

"There were people hit by shrapnel from the bombs but they didn't usually bleed too much because shrapnel is so hot that it cauterizes the wound when it hits you. But, there was this one guy who fell into my trench and said, "Help me!" He held his leg up and he had no knee left. It was all shot up. I had my bandage kit with me. I poured sulfa powder in the wound and bandaged him up, using all of my kit and some from his. I left and got a medical corpsman to take care of him. He took his leg but there was just skin holding it on.

"I don't know what happened to him. It was a hard thing to see, my first taste of combat. I was scared but the sight of that knee just hanging on didn't make me 'urp' or anything."

The A09 pilot, Captain Wray, commandeered a car about 2 p.m. to get his crew the eighty miles back to Nichols Field by land since the Japanese had eliminated flying as an option.

"Boy, I was shook up when we got back. Sergeant Suttle (sic), a friend of mine, saw I was upset so he handed me a bottle of liquor. I didn't normally drink, but took a couple of good swigs. It didn't even faze me. Under normal conditions, I would have been flat on my back!"

The 1st sergeant told the shaken airman to "go down by the hangar, lie down, and relax. Nothing is going to happen tonight."

"Ya! Lie down and relax! Well, about midnight that night Japanese bombers came and clobbered Nichols Field. I was sleeping in the hangar when the first bombs came down. They never rang the siren, but I knew right away what it was and got in one of the ditches that happened to be there. It didn't take me long to get out to that ditch, I'll tell you! After that, we dug foxholes so we were ready for the next time.

"We had sure been caught with our drawers down. That's all there was to it! The Japanese destruction of our airbases shouldn't have happened because we had

Alf Larson sits in the cockpit of a new fighter plane at the Philippine base.

all the indications that war was coming. The Japanese had landed north of us at Lingayen. They bombed Aparri, a town on the northern tip of Luzon. They blasted and obliterated the pursuit base at Iba, about sixty miles west of Clark Field. The bomber commander, Major General Brereton, had gone to MacArthur's headquarters and tried to get permission to take off and bomb the Japanese launching base at Formosa but MacArthur told him, "We are not at war; we are in the state of war." General MacArthur was in charge, so the bombers stayed on the ground.

"Personally, I don't think a bombing mission to Formosa would have succeeded anyway because we weren't really prepared and so many things could have gone wrong. But by now, the Japanese had wrecked everything anyway. On December 9, 1941, they really plastered us. Then they came about noon on December 10, 1941, and just leveled Nichols Field and the Navy Yard at Cavite. And I mean leveled it!

"There had been plenty of bombing and strafing runs between December 10 and 21. They would plaster us with bombs, and then Jap fighters would come down across and strafe us. Each time, you'd jump in a foxhole and listen for the loud whistle streak of the bombs. It was the one you didn't hear coming that would have killed you.

"The bombing could really shake you up. If it was close, your eardrums would burst. So, during heavy bombing and shelling, I would keep my mouth open to equalize the pressure in both sides of my ears. If bombs fall in the distance, you can feel a tremor. If it is close, you 'bounce' because the tremors would lift you up off the ground and drop you again. We bounced over and over as the bombs fell."

There were casualties at both Nichols and Clark fields, but "Clark Field had the most injuries and people killed because the Japanese caught them at lunchtime with their pants down. At Nichols, we had more time to disperse. In fact, we didn't stay in the barracks and were soon bivouacked away from the base about one-half mile, with our field kitchen, in 'the boonies.'"

Perhaps most frustrating to those enduring the bombardments was their inability to do much to their attackers in return.

"The armament we had consisted of old World War I Lewis anti-aircraft guns, the ones with the drum on top of them, and they would jam up! Everything we had over there was World War I stuff, including many rifles. The first airplane ride I took over there was in a ZB3 where the pilot sat in front, the gunner sat in back and everything was open. We were that outdated. The Japanese zeros could fly circles around everything we had over there at that time.

"America knew, should have known, war was coming, but we weren't ready. Some of the P-40 fighters we had didn't have any cooling fluid because it hadn't been shipped with the dang things! So, there they sat. A lot of them were destroyed on the ground because they couldn't take off without cooling fluid. After the raids, a ship came in with the stuff that should have been there in the first place and we could patch up some of them that were left so they could fly."

The Philippines had long been at the bottom of the United States' list where sending new military equipment was concerned. As war began to loom ever closer in the Pacific, however, military leaders started to send more modern equipment to the airstrips, including a batch of P-38 fighter planes originally earmarked for Sweden.

"It was funny really because I never, I mean never, expected to have to use my understanding of Swedish in the Philippines. But, here the planes arrived and all of the mechanical instructions for the airplanes were in Swedish! Since I could still read Swedish, I spent two weeks helping them put the planes together."

Despite the lack of equipment, Philippine airmen did all they could to fight back. Mechanics worked around the clock to keep brave airmen flying against the Japanese. Larson was one of those airmen involved in the desperate battle to defend the Philippines — a struggle that nearly cost him his life on the one bombing mission of his career, on December 21, 1941.

"The 27th Bombardment Squadron had come over without airplanes and had borrowed three obsolete B-18s from Nichols Field to bomb the Japanese at Lingayen, northwest of Manila, where the Japanese had already invaded with little opposition. They didn't have enough qualified crewmembers and asked me to fly with them, and our commander told me to go.

"The Japanese's transports were still anchored in the harbor and we were going to try and sink some of them. It was tough because we didn't have a bomb-sight in the plane, but we dropped the bombs at about 18,000 feet anyway. I don't know if we hit anything, but I saw water splashing.

"On the way home, instead of going straight back to Nichols Field, we made a big circle. At dusk, we weren't far from Lingayen and north of Baguio when the Jap fighters jumped us.

"We spotted the Zeroes when they were some ways off, so we were as ready as we could ever be. All gunners were at their positions and ready to fire when they came at us. We beat off the first attack, but then they split up so that we could not concentrate our fire on them. Soon, it became an individual affair, a sort of one on one deal. On the third pass, one of the Zeroes set fire to our right engine.

"With our engine on fire, the Japanese left, probably because they were running out of fuel and it was getting dark. As soon as he saw they were leaving, our pilot gave the order to bail out. I had never jumped out of an airplane before, and I can tell you that when a person jumps there are two distinct shocks. First you hit the slipstream after leaving the plane. Then, the parachute opens. Both really jolt you.

"It was dark by this time and I was floating above the jungle canopy as it seemed to rise to meet my feet. My landing was not 'textbook.' I landed in a tall pine

Alf Larson and crew work on one of the standard-issue World War I planes the Philippine forces used to defend the island in 1941.

tree with my parachute snagged in its branches. The snagged chute stopped my descent short of the ground, but it also kept me from falling out of the tree. I was extra lucky because I didn't break anything in my 'landing.'

"I climbed into a crotch in the tree which was relatively comfortable. I mean it wasn't exactly a lounge chair, but beggars can't be choosers. I decided to stay in the tree because I couldn't see how high up I was in the dark, and I knew that the jungle canopy could be a hundred feet off of the ground. In fact, in peacetime, we had lost a couple of aircraft in the jungle canopy because it was so dense and high."

Larson spent a tense night huddled in the branches of the tree, some fifty feet off the jungle floor, not knowing how far up he was, if there were enemy troops nearby or how, or if, he would ever get down.

The next morning, a Philippine constabulary, or a member of Philippine troops, found Larson. Filipino scouts also located the rest of the crew, which had scattered closer to Baguio. The scouts then managed to find a car, and the six weary fliers once again traveled by land back home.

This time, the car ride took two days and two nights because the lost airmen had to ride along back roads to avoid detection by Japanese ground troops near the area.

"None of our crew had been injured beyond cuts and scratches, which made the traveling easier. In addition, the Filipinos seemed to know where they could or could not drive to avoid the Japanese. We were still worried, though, because we knew that there were reports of Jap patrols active in the entire area. Friendly Filipinos apparently alerted our driver to the patrols' whereabouts, so we made it back to Nichols Field in one piece."

The tired fliers arrived at Nichols Field December 23 and had little time to rest from their ordeal. The next day, the airmen found themselves at sea as the Army Air Corps began to evacuate Manila and Nichols Field and retreated to the Bataan Peninsula at the southern end of the island.

"The evacuation was near total chaos as we all scrambled around to load the trucks with whatever gear we were able to get together on such short notice. We were taken down to the Manila docks and rode to Bataan on interisland steamers. "We didn't feel like giving up and were angry at the situation more than anything.

 "We didn't think about it being Christmas or anything either. I don't recall having time to think about that at all. It wasn't much of a holiday, but it was my last free Christmas for a long time."

From the steamers Larson was trucked to his new position on the defensive front lines of Bataan because, with fewer than ten aircraft left on the entire island of Luzon, his airman services were no longer needed. By Jan. 2, 1942, Manila Bay was securely in Japanese hands.

In the short period of time since the Japanese invaded, the nearly 12,000 Americans and 62,000 Filipinos on the eighty-mile-wide, thirty-mile-long Bataan Peninsula were organized into three different lines of defense. The Army Air Corps, including Larson's outfit, became infantry and had the east side of the line. At first, Larson was stationed as reserves in and around Pilar, where he waited and patrolled as the Japanese kept pushing the 31st Infantry, the 45th Infantry and the Filipino soldiers back.

Larson's location soon became the front line, or the third and final line of defense.

"We didn't get engaged too many times because our end of the line was much more open geographically, so anything that moved we could see and shoot. The scariest part was the outpost line of resistance we had about 1,000 yards ahead of our main line. We set up alarm devices there — basically cans with rocks on barbed wire. At the outpost line you didn't want to shoot flares, so we'd call back to the main line and they'd shoot flares for us, ahead of our position. We did see Japs on our patrols, but we didn't engage them as we were usually greatly outnumbered."

Patrols proved the more dangerous duty. Larson and a small group of soldiers would sneak through the area for up to four days at a time trying to locate Japanese units and ascertain their strength and positions.

"On most patrols we didn't run across Japanese, however. And, even when we did, we were often too outnumbered to engage them. However, one time five of us heard chattering and saw three Japanese bathing. They didn't even know we were there, and we shot them. It was the first time I hit somebody, and I did not feel any remorse or guilt about it at all. They were the enemy, and I knew that if the roles had been reversed, they'd have done the same as we did. However, in retrospect now, I know that we shot unarmed men but I also know that we were at war and we felt that 'get rid of as many as possible in any way, shape or form' feeling."

Just how dangerous patrols could be became evident soon after Larson's introduction to field combat when a lieutenant he knew, with the 803 Engineers, asked to go out to see what patrol duty was like.

"On their way back, the head of that patrol committed a cardinal sin by not posting lookouts while the patrol was resting to better prevent being caught by surprise by the enemy. Naturally, the enemy jumped them. The Japs killed the lieutenant and left Staff Sergeant Rubinowitz (sic) with a broken leg. The rest of

A depiction of the battles around Clark Field. This is one of many sketches by former POW and Bataan survivor Ben Steele. Sketch courtesy of Ben Steele.

the patrol hid Sergeant Rubinowitz in the brush and beat the Japanese back to our lines.

"I was part of the patrol sent to recover the lieutenant's body and find and return the injured sergeant. We found the wounded man, improvised a stretcher out of two shirts with poles stuck through the arms and sent him back to our lines. We also saw the lieutenant's body at the edge of a cane field and tried to get him. We came under such intense fire in the effort that several of our men were wounded, and we had to give up the attempt. Two other patrols also failed to retrieve the body. The last patrol finally set fire to the cane field and drove the Japanese out of there, killing several of the Japanese as they ran from the burning field. However, the Japanese also took the lieutenant's body away with them, so he was never recovered."

The dangers of combat were many and frequent as

the American and Filipino forces desperately fought to hang onto the Bataan Peninsula and even beat the Japanese back. Such efforts came at a high price, however. For example, only 212 of 600 U.S. soldiers survived a successful counterattack against the Japanese when they tried to land behind American lines Jan. 23, 1942, according to *The History of the United States Naval Operations in World War II.*

The most constant worry for American and Filipino troops was not the Japanese, however. It was food.

As Major Richard M. Gordon (USA Ret.) reports on the Battling Bastards of Bataan web site, troops were cut to half rations in January. By early spring Bataan troops were fighting on 1,000 calories a day, mostly consumed in rice and fish. In addition, as many as three-fourths of the front line American troops were further weakened with bouts of malaria, Gordon notes.

Supplies of all kinds had been running scarce since the start of the Japanese invasion in large part because General MacArthur had said no to "War Plan Orange"— a plan to stock Bataan with six months' supply of food, ammunition, medicine, and supplies — because he did not want to "fight defensively." Instead, MacArthur had sent the bulk of supplies to forward Filipino fighters who were quickly overrun by the Japanese.

In addition to nearly 12,000 American servicemen, "General MacArthur had an impressive army of about 200,000 Filipinos. He had a lot of bodies on paper! But there was little unity among the Filipino troops. For instance, there were nine or ten different dialects in the various Philippine regions. Soldiers were organized with no consideration as to who came from where. They couldn't even converse! It would be like taking a Chinese soldier and putting him in with an American, and neither could speak each other's language.

"Before the war, General MacArthur said, 'My Phil-

ippine army can hold the Japanese at the beaches,'
and ordered the supplies placed on front line positions
around Luzon. But, when the Japanese landed at
Lingayen and the Filipino army couldn't hold their
positions, the Japanese got our food and supplies. As
a result, the Filipino Army was starving and we had a
ration shortage that wouldn't quit.

"We were starving to death, and the Filipinos were
getting less than we were. General MacArthur's inept
planning wasted all the food, so we received half rations or less on Bataan from day one because there
was nothing to eat. We got one cup of rice in the morning and everything else we had to scrounge. We spent
more time looking for food than fighting the Japanese!"

Everything that grew or moved on the island was
fair game for the hungry fighters.

"We ate the jungle. We ate snake, lizard, pony, mule,
iguana, rats, monkeys. You name it; we tried it! We were
told to 'watch the monkeys and eat what they eat.'
Some even ate the monkeys, but monkey is tough to
eat. It's stringy and, if you bake it, it looks like a little
child so that's hard to eat. Snake tasted good though;
it's a white meat. There were carabou too which look
like water buffalo, taste like beef and have the disposi-
tion of a hornet.

"We had little fruit because the front lines were
mostly in sugar cane fields that were open, and the
jungle's lush canopy was hundreds of feet in the air.
On the ground, there was almost no underbrush. We
did find wild bananas though. They tasted good but
have very little meat and a lot of seeds. You could just
chew a bit around the edges and that was it. There
weren't any wells, so we drank water from streams, and
I still don't know why we didn't get sick.

"It got so bad that they slaughtered the cavalry
horses. There were people that wouldn't eat horse

meat, but they suffered in the end. It was the same in prison camp. We killed a snake there, but there were people that wouldn't eat snake. Why? It was eat or die, and they still wouldn't eat it. So, they died."

The Japanese, who had not been resupplied since their invasion, were also starving. As a result, a strange understanding between enemies emerged for a time on the island.

"The town of Pilar had an abandoned sugar refinery and we had an informal arrangement with the Japs. When we passed through on patrol, we would stop and fill our canteens with molasses. When the Japanese passed through, they would stop and get their molasses. This continued until one time our molasses tasted like sulfur. We thought the Japanese had put something in the molasses. We spotted their positions and shelled the heck out of them with our artillery! Eventually we found out it was the darn sugar dregs in the bottom of the vats that were responsible for the taste; it wasn't the Japanese's fault at all. But it ended our arrangement."

GIVING IN

By early spring of 1942, the American defense was desperate indeed. Units were holding up defensive lines in the jungle on the west side of the Bataan Peninsula while service troops like the air corps battled to hold the east side lines. The more intense fighting took place in the open areas and sugar cane fields around the Bataan Air Base, some thirty and eventually just five miles from the front lines.

Filipino troops, charged with holding the center of the line on the Bataan Peninsula, took the worst of the Japanese attacks as the enemy found hole after hole and kept pushing the lines farther and farther toward the end of the peninsula. Eventually, the Filipino regiment just walked away from the Japanese — a move that marked the beginning of the end for the American resistance.

"General King, the man in charge of the Northern Luzon Force, did try to establish a line of resistance but failed. If we would have had food and equipment, we probably could have counter-attacked. We might have been able to push them off Bataan. The Filipinos quit because they were starving to death, and large stores of food had been abandoned to the enemy. I can't fault them because they had it worse then we did, and we had it bad."

After a month teetering on the front lines and enduring several harrowing patrols, Larson's command-ing officer sent the Minnesota enlistee back to Corregidor for one week of rest on the island fortress, located just off the Bataan Peninsula. "I was housed in a hospital wing in Melinta Tunnel while I was there. Most of the patients were old men of field grade officer status (colonel or higher) and were on canes, crutches or in wheelchairs. When they were outside for fresh air and some sunshine, and the Japanese artillery on the Cavite mainland side started shelling Corregidor, these old infirmed officers would panic. Canes, crutches and wheelchairs would go flying. They would race back into the safety of the tunnel. If anyone was in their way, they would just run right over them.

"I knew then that I had to get out of there; it was driving me crazy. I only spent three days of my allot-ted one week R&R on Corregidor. It took me about a week to get reacclimated to front line duty after I got back to my outfit."

Soon after, Larson visited a wounded friend in a hospital on Bataan — a gesture that proved fortuitous for the battle weary airman.

"In late January of 1942, I went to visit a friend from the 27th Material Squadron who had dengue fever, which is similar to malaria. He was in Hospital #2, which was about 30 miles south of Pilar in southern Bataan. He was recovering nicely, but others in the hospital were not so lucky.

"I think now that most of those men in the hospi-tals (#1 and #2) did not survive after the surrender when the Japanese forced them out of the hospital and forced them to walk and endure what we did. They were already weakened from wounds and disease, and sur-viving all of that would have been nearly impossible. I suppose that some patients did survive it, but I've never found out for sure."

This monument is one of the Death March memorials at Kilometer 00 Park near Mariveles, where the march began in 1942. Photo courtesy of Rick Peterson.

During his visit, Larson bumped into another friend, Colonel George. "He was there visiting an injured airman and we talked. He asked where I was stationed and I told him 'at the front lines.' He didn't say anything else to me but, about two days later, my first sergeant came by and said, 'Pack your bags. You're going back to Bataan Air Base.'

Larson stayed at his new post for the next three months. Though he no longer faced the dangers of front-line fighting, no station on Bataan was safe anymore.

"A Japanese observation flight would come over every morning. We called him 'Washing Machine Charlie' because we could hear his plane knocking and rumbling before he ever came over. After he had flown over, the bombers and strafers would come. We got bombed and strafed every single day!"

While many men were wounded by bombing shrapnel at the air base, there were not the numbers of gunshot and artillery — as well as bombing — shrapnel wounds that Larson had witnessed on the front lines.

Despite gallant attempts to hold the peninsula and even push the Japanese back, the Japanese forces proved too great, and the American and Filipino supplies too low. On March 11, 1942, President Franklin Roosevelt ordered General MacArthur to evacuate himself to Australia, leaving Lt. Gen. Jonathan Wainwright in charge of all Philippine forces from his base on the island of Corregidor and Maj. Gen. Edward P. King in charge of the troops fighting with him on the Bataan Peninsula.

On April 3, Japanese General Masaharu Homma made his final push to seize the Bataan Peninsula and what remained of the Philippine islands.

On April 9, 1942, Major General King decided to surrender his forces rather than see his men slaughtered by the conquering Japanese.

"He just couldn't see any reason to continue. He didn't have authority from Wainwright, his commanding officer on Corregidor, to surrender. I wasn't there but my friend Tony Urban (sic) was there when General King told the soldiers that, "Men, I know you feel bad, but you didn't surrender. I surrendered you."

Despite the writing on the wall and the starvation and exhaustion they were suffering, most fighting men were not happy to hear about the surrender.

"That night I was mad because I couldn't figure out why we had to stop fighting. There were a lot of people who would like to have kept on. But it was no use; we had no defense."

Many men felt abandoned by their leader General MacArthur, who had failed to supply them adequately and then left the island in retreat. And, many felt abandoned by their country, which was not rallying to their cause. American War correspondent Frank Hewlett captured the soldiers' thoughts in a poem that spread through the units like wildfire: called *The Battling Bastards of Bataan*. It was a verse Larson and his buddies so identified with that he remembers it still. It reads, in part:

> *We are the Battling Bastards of Bataan,*
> *No Mama, no Papa, no Uncle Sam!*
> *No Aunts, no Uncles, no Cousins, no Nieces,*
> *No Planes, no Pills, no Artillery Pieces!*
> ***And Nobody gives a Damn!***

"That was a pretty accurate assessment of our situation and it was traumatic to know that we were through. Then worse thoughts began to sink in. After I got mad I got scared because you began to realize, 'we're going to surrender to the enemy, what's going to happen to us now?'"

While sporadic fighting continued as General King negotiated the surrender, most troops obeyed his order to quit fighting. And, they began to destroy equipment and supplies so the Japanese wouldn't benefit from them.

"Everything was chaos, I'll tell you! We burned as much as we could … equipment, materials, our personal gear, or anything the Japanese could use. What didn't burn was thrown into the ocean or wherever we could get rid of it. I had a watch and a class ring. My folks had given me the watch for graduation from high school. My ring was my high school graduation class ring. The night of the surrender, I threw both of them in a creek so nobody could find the damned things. They would have taken them off of me anyway. In fact, later on during the march, I saw Japanese soldiers who had three or four wristwatches on their forearms. I knew darned well where they came from!

"I took my 45-caliber revolver, wrapped it in rags, put it in a can, and dumped a bunch of oil on it to protect it. I put it in the hollow of a tree. I'll bet it's still there. And, anyone that had any Japanese stuff — swords, yen, or anything scrounged from dead Japanese — had to get rid of it. You didn't dare have any of that on you. If the Japanese found it, you were finished!

Larson and about fifty others from various units began walking toward the Japanese lines, toward Mariveles. Even that more leisurely walk toward their fate was not without surprises.

"About two miles from Mariveles we stopped at a supply camp, which had an ammunition dump. American troops had recently been there and, to our surprise, the kitchen still had food in it. We had C-rations, which were items packaged in cans that you could cook and D-rations, which were absolutely dry foods that usually consisted of a chocolate bar with oatmeal and other nutrients. At this point, we had very little of anything. Even after we had surrendered, this knucklehead lieutenant wanted to ration the food we had!

"We also found a bunch of World War I hand grenades. We told the lieutenant these had to be destroyed so the Japanese wouldn't get them. He tried to stop us, but we wouldn't listen to him. We found a slit trench, pulled the pins, and threw them in. Half of them wouldn't even go off! That was the quality of the stuff we had. We were fighting World War II with World War I equipment — literally!"

While this particular lieutenant earned little respect, Larson admits he owes him a debt of gratitude.

"One of his decisions saved my life. I knew a planter down on the island of Mindoro, which is quite a ways south of Manila. We had visited him many times and stayed at his ranch. We found out he had a guerrilla operation going on, and two of us wanted to get a dug-out and go. Our chicken-shit lieutenant said, 'Absolutely not. The Japanese know how many dugouts and men we have.' He said we had to stay put because the Japanese controlled and patrolled everything all the way down. As I look back I realize there was probably no way in heck we could have made it; I probably would have been killed."

As Larson and the men at Mariveles waited for their new lives as prisoners of war to begin, they could hear the last ditch attempts of Lt. Gen. Jonathan Wainright and thousands of American soldiers trying to hold the island fortress of Corrigedor, some three miles off the southern tip of Bataan. Those final defenders would not resign to the same, now inevitable, fate as their Bataan comrades for nearly a month. Then, on May 6, 1942, Lieutenant General Wainwright surrendered the forces on Corregidor and, after the war, was awarded the Congressional Medal of Honor for gallant efforts to hold back the Japanese.

"There were thousands of soldiers on Corregidor, mostly Americans, and for quite a while we could hear their guns blasting away at the Japanese. The problem with the Corregidor defenses was that all their coastal artillery guns, except the mortars, were trained seaward, so they couldn't swivel them around and fire inland which is where the Japanese were. So, all they could use to hit the Japanese on Bataan were big 12- to 24-inch mortars.

Though they knew the fate of Corregidor still hung in the balance, Larson and his buddies were more concerned with their individual future.

"We were just sitting and waiting. We knew it was inevitable, only a matter of time. But waiting for anything — a fight, the surrender, whatever — was sometimes worse than going through it. You were on pins and needles wondering what would happen, imagining what could happen, though we never really imagined what the march turned out to be. We thought that they would honor the Geneva Convention rules for treating prisoners of war. We never believed they would torture and execute us. Still, we were apprehensive, wondering, waiting. The not knowing is always the worst, and we relearned this many times as POWs: Anticipation is usually worse than Participation.'"

As the ragtag group came to a rest at Mariveles, Mother Nature provided a foreshadowing of the shaky existence they were about to enter as prisoners of war, Larson recalls.

"We stopped to rest because we were exhausted. All of a sudden the whole earth started quivering under us. It was a damned earthquake, and were we shocked!"

After about three days of waiting on pins and needles, a Japanese combat patrol walked into the camp.

"I remember what I felt was sort of a relief. It was just 'ahhhh, it's over.'"

"The patrol had an interpreter who could speak danged good English. He told us that the next morning we would be heading toward our place of captivity. He didn't say where. He said we would be fed.

"That was good to hear because, though we didn't know what would happen to us now or how we would be treated, we really didn't think they would torture or execute us. Besides, our main concern was still food and he had promised we would be fed. Technically we were fed, though it was next to nothing (one cup of rice) and it was many days and miles later."

Larson's captivity got off to an especially bad start when a Japanese private picked up one of the American 45-caliber pistols.

"I don't know where he found it, but he sure didn't

know how to handle the danged thing because he shot and killed himself with it. They hauled him off and chattered like a bunch of monkeys. For a while we thought they would reprimand us but nothing happened. We got ready to move out."

The next morning, April 12, 1942, Larson joined some 7,500 to 10,000 Americans and up to 65,000 Filipinos lining up on the roads of the Bataan Peninsula. (The exact number of prisoners can never be ascertained because no records were kept of how many were killed or escaped in the final days of the battle before the surrender).

Together, these fighters took the first nervous steps of a horrifyingly grueling seventy-five to eighty mile walk to San Fernando — the forced hike that became the "Bataan Death March."

MARCHING ON

"**W**e were to walk eighty miles in six days. That doesn't seem very far, I guess, but we were in such awful condition that eighty miles was a heck of a long way to walk. The Bataan Death March lasted just six days, but a lot happened in six days.

"On the first day, I saw two things I will never forget. A Filipino man had been beheaded. His body lay on the ground with blood everywhere. His head was a short distance away. Then I saw a dead Filipino woman with her legs spread apart and her dress pulled up over her. She obviously had been raped and there was a bamboo stake in her private area. These are instances I would like to forget but cannot forget."

By the end of the first day — without food or water and in daytime temperatures of 105 degrees Fahrenheit — the marching column of soldiers quickly became a nearly subhuman line of staggering forms, fighting thirst, fear, torture, diarrhea, heat and their own minds to somehow keep walking. After all, to stop was to die.

"If people fell down and couldn't go any further, the Japanese would either bayonet or shoot them. They also would bayonet prisoners who couldn't keep up.

"Those who stepped out of line or fell out of ranks were beaten with clubs and/or rifle butts. I found out later that the Japanese would take these prisoners' dog tags off and leave their bodies along the roadside, which was probably the only humanitarian thing they

> "Guys around me dropped but if you tried to help them you'd get beat up or killed. After a while, you just went blank and you became a machine, a walking machine."

did … unless they were just taking a guy's tags so no one could identify him."

"Some American prisoners who couldn't keep up were run over by Japanese vehicles. I saw the remains of an American soldier who had been run over by a tank. I didn't see the actual event, but the Japanese just left his remains in the middle of the road. We could see them as we walked by. He was just flattened out. He had no head; his skull was smashed completely into little pieces. All his bones were smashed, ground up. He was just flat.

"Guys around me dropped but if you tried to help them you'd get beat up or killed. After a while, you just went blank and you became a machine, a walking machine."

The machine moved in groups of a hundred men, staggering along the road four columns wide and marching, with little to no food, water or rest, for five to ten days.

"In the morning, we would get up and start walking. We walked all day. At night, the Japanese took us to a field to sleep. You would lie down and pass out right there."

But the night did not always provide the rest the prisoners so desperately needed.

"The Japanese would make us march anytime. For example, we were put in the field at the end of the day and, just after we got comfortable and settled down, they would come and tell us to get up. We would start out marching again. If they got us up in the middle of the night, we would march the rest of the night and all the next day until night."

The wounded were expected to keep up like everyone else, regardless of their condition. Men who had been hospitalized at the time of the surrender were expected to march as well; most would not survive. When wounded, exhausted or ill prisoners couldn't go on, they were bayoneted, beaten with clubs and rifle butts, and/or shot. To save bullets, or just for the torture of it, the Japanese often skewered prisoners with the ends of their bayonets, scrambling their intestines and sparking nervous twitches through their bodies as the prisoners died.

The Japanese had so-called Buzzard Squads that followed along behind the column and finished off those who couldn't keep up. "I didn't see them because they were behind us. We heard them, though. It was their

POW artist Ben Steele depicts the desperate swallows of Death March hikers quenching their thirst with the stagnant water of a mud hole. Sketch courtesy of the Ben Steele collection.

Filipinos re-enact the Bataan Death March for the 60th anniversary. Photo courtesy of Rick Peterson.

job to 'take care of' any stragglers or those who fell out and couldn't continue. They 'took care of them' by killing them. We could hear the shots and knew another prisoner was dead."

Being surrounded by death was only one form of torture. Some days the Japanese would actually stop the column for an hour and allow the prisoners to sit down for a so-called rest. But the sun baked, open field they forced their prisoners to sit in brought no relaxation. Prisoners soon called this heat torture test the Oriental Sun Treatment and endured it in various forms throughout their captivity.

"If there was any shade, the Japanese found it. We just sat there, the hot sun beating down on us like mad and the guards still walking around, eyeing us. Like some soldiers, I was fortunate because I had my helmet on. If you didn't have a hat on the march, it was tougher. After an hour or so in the field, they would get us up and we would start walking again in the hot sun."

The hike's pace gradually slowed as the prisoners' condition worsened and even the Japanese, who walked alongside their American charges, tired.

"It wasn't a fast pace, just kind of shuffling along. We had been starved for such a long time that we were really run down. We looked like a bunch of stragglers. If we got below a certain walking speed, they would start hollering but, as long as you kept a fairly decent pace, they didn't say or do anything."

The eighty-mile walk would have been inhuman enough for the half-starved surrenderers, but the Japanese's seemingly random forms of torture — in addition to the cruel acts of violence perpetuated against some marchers and Filipino villagers — pushed the prisoners past the point of endurance.

"The Japanese code was that if you surrendered, you were nothing. Anyone who surrendered lost all face, and very few Japanese soldiers ever surrendered. They died or even killed themselves first. So when the Japanese looked at us — at those who'd surrendered to their enemy rather than fight to the death — we were nothing to them. And, that's how they treated us, like nothing worthy of any human compassion or even basic human essentials."

The Japanese had grossly underestimated the number of prisoners they would have to care for and did not consider how sick many of them would be, thinking they would have about 25,000 instead of 75,000 prisoners between American and Filipino troops. Still, most of the horrors suffered along the Death March can be attributed to enormous cultural differences, relayed from the top down, that began and ended with the Japanese contempt for any soldier who did not fight to the death.

Historian Hampton Sides adds in his book *Ghost Soldiers* that the Japanese "had reason to hate the Americans for holding out so long (since Tokyo had expected Bataan to fall months earlier), and they had reason to

In this sketch called "The Stragglers," POW artist Ben Steele depicts the final moments of a fallen marcher's life. Those who collapsed along the road were killed. Sketch courtesy of the Ben Steele collection.

hate the Americans for giving up so soon (since according to the Bushido Code, surrender was beneath the dignity of a true soldier)."

In his book *Surrender and Survival*, E. Bartlett Kerr explains that the Japanese code was only one cultural difference that contributed to the horrors the POWs experienced. "Crowding was a part of Japanese efficiency" as was physical punishment. "It was routine for a superior to strike or beat a subordinate for minor infractions (in the Japanese military) ... mass punishment was not unusual." In addition, Kerr adds that the Japanese had long considered Americans to be "pleasure seeking, soft and materialistic." In other words, they looked down upon them as racially soft as well as militarily soft for surrendering.

In addition, according to Elizabeth Marie Himchak in her research for the *Bataan Project,* military orders instructed Japanese guards to "...supervise their charges rigidly, taking care not to become obsessed with mistaken ideas of humanitarianism or swayed by personal feelings towards prisoners..."

All of this aggravated the horrors of the Death March, adds Col. Irving Alexander in his book, *Surviving Bataan & Beyond.* "The vast differences between the American and Japanese in language, temperament, customs, manners, training and discipline, all combined to create a colossal misunderstanding. The half-starved American prisoners were clubbed, bayoneted and subjected to countless indignities in an unsuccessful effort to fit them into what the Oriental mind conceived as the appropriate mold for captives of war."

Japanese guards repeatedly tried new ways to mold and punish their captors.

Most often, they denied the prisoners food and water, and even taunted them with the food and water that surrounded them. For four days, Larson's column of marchers ate nothing and drank only ditch water, if they could even get to it.

"There was good water all around us. Artesian wells were flowing everywhere, but they would not let us go and get it. Men went stark raving mad! Soldiers broke ranks and ran towards the water. They went completely insane because they had to get it. They never got it! Of course, you know what happened to them; they were shot before they reached the water.

"I remember the first day our guard stopped the march. You could hear and see a good flowing stream about 100 to 150 feet away. We could see and hear the water, and we just stood there listening to it. He never let us get any."

Stagnant water that pooled along the trail in ditches and puddles — that the carabao used to douse flies from their backs — was the prisoners' only way to quench their thirst, if they could scoop the precious infested water from its hole without falling out of line.

"We drank foul smelling and stagnant water from the ditches. You scooped it up as you walked. We were not allowed to go to the artesian wells, which were about half a block from the road. Fortunately, I didn't get any ill effects from drinking it, but some guys got terrible diarrhea.

"If anyone had to relieve themselves, they couldn't stop marching. They went right in their drawers as they walked. If you stopped or got off to the side, you would have been bayoneted or shot. I didn't go to the bathroom because I had nothing to pass. My body fluid came out in sweat, and I don't recall going to the bathroom until we got up to Camp O'Donnell. The first time I urinated, I thought I was going to die; it burned like sin."

Some prisoners, Larson included, were able to actually sneak away from the fields at night and fill a canteen or two with artesian well water. It was a risky move.

"You didn't dare get too many canteens or they would rattle. We would handle them very carefully and quietly sneak off to an artesian well. You held a canteen under water and filled two or three of them. Then we came back and passed them around. If the Japanese had caught us, that would have been it! We would have been shot."

Food was more difficult to sneak. In fact, most prisoners — already starved from the lack of supplies before the surrender — had no food of any kind for four or more days.

"Along the way, Filipinos would try to give us food, and the Japanese killed some of them for it. I personally never saw any of the food they tossed reach anybody, but the Filipinos did try to help us.

"I have a lot of respect for most Filipinos. The Japa-

Those re-enacting the Death March portray the Japanese contempt for their prisoners as part of a 60th anniversary event in the Philippines. Photo by Rick Peterson.

nese treated them like dirt, a lot worse than they treated us. On the march, civilians would show us "V" for victory signs with their fingers, shout encouragement, and try and throw us rice balls and banana leaves. If a guard was right there, the food would be taken away, we'd be beaten and the Filipino would probably be shot. They knew that and they still tried to get food to us. I'm not sure that all of them loved America so much as they hated the Japanese and what the Japanese were doing to them, and to us."

Taking away the promise of food was one of the Japanese's favorite forms of torture, on the walk and later in captivity.

"During the day, the Japs would tell us we would get rice balls when we got to our nighttime destination. When we got to the field where we were going to spend the night, you could see and smell their food cooking across the road. Then they would give some excuse why we couldn't have any. I don't remember exactly what the excuses were, but they usually had to do with some phony rule infraction on our part. Anyway, they would eat the food in front of us, but we wouldn't get any. I remember this happened at least two times on the march. Finally, the last two nights, everyone got one rice ball each day to eat. Each ball of rice would have filled one coffee cup."

In between the starvation, diarrhea and perpetual walking, the marchers bore witness to some of the most inhuman acts of violence ever perpetrated.

"Some Japanese seemed to take special delight in torturing us. I don't remember what day it was because things were kind of hazy on the trip. On the march out of Bataan, a Japanese cavalryman was standing in the middle of the road swinging a baseball bat. He didn't care who he hit. He just kept swinging that bat! When I walked by, that bat caught me across my upper left leg. Boy, did it hurt! I kept going because I didn't want to let that son-of-a-gun — I could use stronger language — know that he had hurt me. That was the only bad

> "For all the Japs did to us, they could never take away our thoughts, our silent prayers. Sometimes that was all we had left, and it was the most important thing."

thing that happened to me personally on the march, thank God."

Japanese army trucks heading further into the peninsula often brushed past the marchers. The close proximity offered passing Japanese soldiers the chance to strike out at the enemy, Larson recalls, noting soldiers would often lean out of the trucks and hit prisoners with the ends of rifles.

In *Death March: The Survivors of Bataan*, Sgt. Ralph Levenberg recalls witnessing similar incidents. "They'd be riding on the back of a truck and would have these long black snake whips. They'd whip that thing out and get some poor bastard by the neck or torso and drag him behind their truck. 'Course if one of our guys was quick enough, he didn't get dragged too far. But if the Japs got a sick guy…'"

Generally speaking, the Japanese did not perform mass executions on the march. However, there were cases including a report that several Japanese guards bound the hands of hundreds of Filipino soldiers and decapitated each of them with a sword, one at a time.

Few saw such mass atrocities along the march, however. For most marchers, one of the most horrifying scenes was witnessing the Japanese bury a man alive. "On one occasion I saw a soldier who had diarrhea really bad and went over to a ditch to go to the bathroom. After he finished, he could barely get up. He slipped and fell backwards into the trench. The Japanese ordered a prisoner detail to cover him up right there, which they did. The detail had no choice!"

Horror was everywhere the marchers turned. "As we walked along, we could see the bodies of decomposing American soldiers and Filipino women who had been mutilated and obviously raped. I'm sure the dogs in the area got fat!

"I'll tell you, everything you have read or heard about those little yellow slant-eyes happened on the march! After the march was over, I didn't see any men buried alive, I didn't see that level of torture."

In fact, the only way to withstand all that Larson did see was to block it out as much as possible and keep hoping and praying that somehow he would endure another step, another day.

"Once the march started, everything just sort of froze in my mind. I was pretty numb the whole time. I didn't think; I didn't feel. I was like a robot and just kept moving. Other than daylight or dark, I lost all track of time.

"I had to blank everything out and focus straight ahead. Everything just went blank, and I put one foot in front of the other over and over and over again. I lived from day to day, hour by hour, minute by minute.

This stone plaque marks the site of the Capas train station where the march ended. Photo by Rick Peterson.

The San Fernando train station now stands empty on silent tracks that belie the horrors borne upon the rails during the Bataan Death March. Photo by Rick Peterson.

The only thing I thought about was the moment and that, 'The good Lord willing, I'll get through the day.'

"What I didn't say was, 'Lord, if you get me out of this, I'll go to church every Sunday.' There were people that did, some that hadn't seen the inside of a church since heaven knows when. Before the war I heard people say, 'I don't believe in religion; I don't believe in God.' Well, after the war started, I never met an atheist. When the bombs started falling and shells started whistling, they got religion in a hurry. The old saying from World War I, 'There are no atheists in the foxhole' is a good, honest statement and pretty darn true."

Faith in God carried Larson through the worst of the march and prison camp. And, as hard as it was to hold on to anything, Larson never let go of God.

"I carried a little pocket Testament with me the whole time and read it regularly. That's one thing the Japanese didn't take away from me! I carried it between my legs in my shorts on the march, and I still have it. I will always believe that that little Bible helped me a great deal. But I don't think it made a life or death difference to me because even if they had taken it away, I still would have had the 23rd Psalm — which remains my favorite — and silently prayed for His will to be done. I would have still kept saying, as I did, 'Lord, whatever your will is, help me endure it.' For all the Japs did to us, they could never take away our thoughts, our silent prayers. Sometimes that was all we had left, and it was the most important thing."

Attitude was everything on the march and in the prison camp, Larson adds. "A man who could get within himself and talk to and entertain himself within his own mind, that was the man who, with a little luck, survived."

On the sixth day of the march, the column of shadow soldiers reached San Fernando and what looked like a brief respite. They would not be walking farther, it seemed, as a train was waiting to carry them about sixty miles to the Camp O'Donnell prisoner camp.

"At first I was relieved because I thought at least we wouldn't have to walk anymore, but I soon found out what was in store for us. The train consisted of six or seven World War I boxcars — forty- by-eights, I guess they called them. Right away, they began cramming us into boxcars, about a hundred men to a car. We were packed so tight that we could only stand and not move at all. There was no jockeying for position because we could hardly move. We could not even fall down and were held upright by the shear mass of bodies. Then, they shut the door.

"It was nearly summer and hotter than Billy Blazes! The stench was terrible because some men had diarrhea and could only relieve themselves by going in their drawers and subsequently going on the men packed around them like sardines. The only ventilation came from whatever cracks there were in the boxcars. We were on the train from early morning until late afternoon without getting out. As I recall, three men died in our car; they died just standing there next to someone."

In *Death March: The Survivors of Bataan*, Cpl. Hubert Gater also recalls the torturous train ride in the oven the Japanese had crammed him into. "The three hours were almost indescribable. Men fainting with no place to fall. Those with dysentery had no control of themselves. As the car swayed, the urine, sweat and vomit rolled three inches deep back and forth around and in our shoes."

As if the dead standing rigid with the suffocating weren't enough, the Japanese stopped the train to seemingly torture their captives further.

"I don't know why, but the train stopped at a little town outside Clark Field, called Angeles. They opened the boxcar doors and the Filipinos tried to feed us. The Japanese beat them off with clubs and shut the boxcar doors. The Filipinos tried to throw the food since they couldn't get close to the train, but we never got the food. After about an hour, the train started up."

Finally, the train squealed to a stop in Capus, near the POWs' final destination.

"We handed out the bodies and then men just stumbled out of the box cars like dominoes. No one rushed out into the fresh air; no one had the strength to rush."

The weary prisoners were given no relief and began marching as soon as a line was formed. This time the distance was shorter. Seven kilometers later, Larson and the several thousand prisoners who had survived the boxcars arrived at the Camp O'Donnell Concentration Camp north of Manila.

Thousands more men would follow as the long line

of death marches ground to a halt the last week of April 1942. By then, an estimated one thousand Americans and ten thousand Filipinos had died on the March, Larson recalls.

"People often think that there was one Death March, that we were a close-knit group, but that's not how it worked. When the Japanese got a bunch together, say one hundred or so, that group would start walking. So it wasn't one long line. One group would start and then a couple of days later, another one came along. When we got to our destination, Camp O'Donnell, soldiers kept coming in. For how long or how many had passed before and after us, I don't know."

MAKING CAMP

From the transitory nightmare of the boxcars, the prisoners entered the new hell they would know as home in Japanese concentration camps.

Larson's first stop was Camp O'Donnell, or Camp Death, a former Filipino military base. The one-square-mile base had been built to house 9,000, but by the time the marchers had arrived, it was packed with more than 50,000 prisoners.

The men in charge of that hell were Captain Yoshio Tsuneyoshi, whom prisoners nicknamed Little Hitler, and his sadistic guard, The Scarecrow.

"They were real SOBs who enjoyed making us as miserable as possible. They made us stand in the hot sun for two hours. They had built a platform by the camp gates just for the captain so he could be above everyone else. He would stand on that thing and give a long harangue through an interpreter to all arriving POWs. He would say we were not recognized as prisoners of war. We were nothing! The Japanese were going to fight this war for a thousand years."

While the captain talked, the dehydrated, hungry and sick prisoners baked in the hot sun for two hours.

The conditions of the camp were as bad as they'd already faced and then some, the prisoners soon discovered.

The camp housed but a few buildings and no beds, and those had quickly been established as hospital barracks. That meant already weakened POWs slept on the concrete ground, open to the elements.

Only thin barbed wire surrounded the camp, but that and some guards were all the Japanese needed to keep the Americans from escaping. The POWs knew that escape would be useless — and eventually deadly — if anyone without trustworthy outside contacts among the Filipinos simply made a run for it.

"The barbed wire around the place was loosely patrolled. I could have gotten out any time, but where would I go? Without outside contacts, I would have been a dead duck because the Japanese offered a hundred-pound sack of rice to any Filipino that would turn in an escaped prisoner. And the Filipinos were starving so badly that they'd take it to save their families."

The Japanese showed little brutality in the enforcement of the boundaries or the rules during Larson's short stay at Camp O'Donnell. "To my knowledge there was not anyone tortured at Camp O'Donnell, at least in our section."

"We did have to acknowledge every single Japanese from the lowest to the highest with a bow. And, you had better bow because if you didn't they would club you, especially if the guards were a private or private first class. They really liked the idea of someone bowing to them, of having power, and many of them wielded it fiercely.

"We had nicknames for many of the guards, like The Scarecrow. Others I remember were The Snake and The Toad, and we called the Japanese flag (a red circle with a white background) the 'flaming red asshole.' Making up names gave us a laugh once in a while, and you could call a guard by the name so long as he didn't speak English. Some of the guys went so far as to bow and smile to Japanese guards while saying, 'Good morning, shit face!' You could usually get away with this because most of the Japanese guards didn't understand English. But you still had to be careful because if they caught you, look out! A beating was coming."

The Camp O'Donnell guards mostly left Larson alone. What torture remained during Larson's stay was of the subtler, more maddening variety.

The American side of Camp O'Donnell had just one water spigot for about 7,500 men, when it functioned. Oftentimes for spite or punishment or both, the Japanese guards would turn off the water to the spigot and the starving prisoners would have to go thirsty as well.

The stronger prisoners helped the weaker get the precious water, Larson recalls. "Instead of each prisoner standing in line to fill his canteen, the more able men would gather as many canteens as they could possibly carry and then distribute the water to the owners of the canteens. Many times the people in line to fill the canteens would be forced to wait all night for the water to be turned back on, however."

Still, Larson adds, the American POWs had drinkable water. The conditions on the Filipino side of Camp O'Donnell were much worse. "The poor Filipinos had to drink polluted river water, and consequently they died like flies."

Larson's short stay at Camp O'Donnell required little of him. There was none of the hard labor the prisoners would endure later on.

"We didn't have to work in the camp itself other than try to keep it sanitary. Each group of prisoners of varying number (from fifty to a hundred) had their own kitchen and was served in their own area. Our food consisted of a thin rice gruel, which we called lugao. We ate once a day, usually at noon. Everyone got a cup of that gruel. It was rice that was thinned out with water so you could pour the stuff."

There was little the prisoners could do to improve

their situation physically. "There was no food to scrounge for because everything had been stripped before we came. Then, on the march, the Japanese had stripped our doctors of everything. We had absolutely no medical supplies and were not given any, no bandages, no ointments and certainly no antibiotics.

"People who needed some type of medical treatment didn't bother to go to the so-called infirmary because we knew there was nothing to treat you with. If you got real bad you were put in the death ward — Zero Ward. Those who went there stayed until they died."

A great many POWs met that fate. More than 1,600 Americans and an estimated 25,000 Filipinos died in the first forty days at Camp O'Donnell alone, Major Gordon reports.

When POWs died at Camp O'Donnell, the bodies were taken to a section of camp away from the main living area that served as a designated burial plot. Prisoners serving on burial details at Camp O'Donnell were burying up to fifty to a hundred men a day in mass graves that were ten to twelve feet long and five feet deep, according to *The Bataan Death March: A Collaborative Project*. The dead were brought to the graves in blankets strung between two shoulder-carried poles. They were then dumped in the graves and covered with dirt. However, ensuing monsoon rains would often bring bodies back to the surface where maggots and dogs feasted on the remains.

The memory of prisoners' bodies floating in the mud remains a lasting image in Larson's mind. "Some of their limbs would protrude from the ground in the rain, a hand or foot sticking up from the mud, and the POWs on burial duty would have to stick them back under, or bury them again. I was fortunate that I was never put on burial duty. It would have been a hard thing to bear.

"Still, the POWs grew hardened to the task of burial, though it affected us if it was somebody that we knew or had been close to at one time or another. But, the Japanese didn't seem to care one way or another if we lived or died."

There was little to take a POW's mind off of his condition and the condition of those around him.

"You couldn't spend time looking for food because there was no food. Everyone eventually got together in small groups with people they knew before the surrender, though there was not much talking because there wasn't much to talk about. I hung around some individuals who had been in my squadron at Nichols Field, such as George Nord, James Whitmore and William Langfitt. George and William survived the whole prison camp episode but James died at one of the other details, in Las Pinas I believe."

What talking there was hardly centered on the usual serviceman's banter of girls waiting in the next port.

"Everything was devoted to food. Guys would talk about seeing a beautiful woman walking down the street with a basket of bananas on her head and all they could think about was, 'God I want those bananas!' When you thought of a woman, you thought of her stirring gravy or serving food; you never thought about sex.

"Other than that, there was nothing to do. We had no writing paper, nothing to read and nothing to think about. A few times you might catch yourself thinking about home, but you tried not thinking about it too often. I tried concentrating on doing math problems in my head to keep my mind busy. You could sleep all day and night if you wanted to but, again, it was not a good idea to become too lethargic mentally or physically. After a few days, people were starting to go crazy because you just had to suffer in silence."

"Rats were never a problem, however. If anyone saw a rat, they caught it and ate it."

The battle the prisoners were now raging with their own minds would prove the most important fight they would face. In the end, prisoners who lost the mental battle between maintaining the will to go on and giving in to the temptation of despair lost their lives.

An early case in point, Larson recalls, were the prisoners who bought into rampant rumors of salvation that circulated around the camp.

"We started hearing harebrained rumors on a daily basis. They were flying everywhere, mostly from people who came back to the camp from work details who didn't actually see what things the rumors were about but were just hopeful they would happen. For example, someone would come in and say, 'There is a Red Cross ship in the harbor with food,' or 'there is another ship and we are going to be exchanged,' or 'we are going to be repatriated very soon.'

"These rumors were really rough on morale. If you listened to all that malarkey, you would go insane. I started to pay attention to them, and they got to me. I reached the point where I just screamed inside that, 'I'm not going to stay here and take this!' But, then where was I going to go? What was the alternative?

"No matter how tempting, a person just had to find a way to push such rumors from one's mind and find a way to endure the place they were in. Still, some prisoners believed the rumors. When they didn't come true, these men became despondent and many of them died, not of starvation or disease, but of shattered hopes."

Prisoners at Camp O'Donnell, then, existed moment to moment, clinging to the remnants of their sanity and health.

Most important to their immediate survival, the prisoners continued to do what they could to fight off the death ward.

"We worked to keep things as clean as possible. Occasionally, we would dig a slit trench for toilet facilities. A slit trench is a long trench you straddle and go to the bathroom in with no privacy. Once a trench was full, it was covered up and we dug another one someplace else.

"Still, all sanitary conditions were practically nil. If you were able to go to the toilet, you used tufts of grass if you could find them. Otherwise, too bad. The only time you could wash was when it rained. Rats were never a problem, however. If anyone saw a rat, they caught it and ate it."

Enduring the conditions at Camp O'Donnell was such a constant battle that the Japanese started transferring prisoners out to work details at other camps throughout the Philippines. To escape the Camp O'Donnell conditions, Larson volunteered for a 200-POW detail the Japanese were forming.

"I didn't know what the detail was and I didn't care; all that mattered was that it got me out of Camp O'Donnell. I later heard that even the Japanese eventually closed Camp O'Donnell down because the facilities were not adequate."

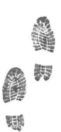

LABORING HARD

Though it felt like a lifetime, Larson had actually spent less than a month at Camp O'Donnell before he and the other prisoners in his new detail were trucked to the former American air base of Clark Field at the end of May 1942, just about the time that the men who had surrendered on Corregidor were arriving at Philippine prison camps.

What was left of the base that Larson had visited at the onset of the war was again home to what was left of America's soldiers.

For one and half years Larson endured the daily work regimen the Japanese had devised — a routine broken only by illness, torture, and eventually, the slow but steady progress of other American troops retaking the Philippines.

"There wasn't much left standing at Clark Field after the Japanese had bombed it (earlier in the war), so they put us in these long bamboo huts, which Filipino Scouts had used before the war. Because of all the bombing damage, there were lots of materials to be scrounged up, and the Japanese let us keep what we could carry back when we were out on cleanup details."

The Clark Field accommodations seemed like paradise compared to the open sewer style camp the prisoners had just left.

"Everyone was able to get hold of a bunk, a mattress, and some blankets. And, we could keep clean because cold running water was available all the time. We even had flush toilets, which functioned throughout our stay at Clark Field. The toilets were not in individual stalls or such but were just a row of seats, like old outhouse seats, with constantly running water in a trough underneath. We also had a section of the toilet house that had showerheads, so that we could take a shower. It was just cold water, but we showered anyway to keep clean and it worked just fine. That was the most fortunate thing to our survival at Clark Field because it increased our morale and sanitation. People felt clean and better and when morale is better, you can focus more on the positive and you stay healthier and stronger."

The prisoners at Clark Field knew they were lucky to have running water and roofs over their heads, luckier than others who had endured the Death March and were housed in other Philippine camps. "Clark Field was one of the best-maintained concentration camps in the whole danged island group. We had people come in from Camp Cabanatuan and other camps, and everyone said Clark Field was the best one of all — of course, the best of the worst was like being in purgatory instead of hell."

Still, by POW standards, things were looking up at Clark Field, even from the beginning. The prisoners' introduction to their new home was almost festive, complete with a pig roast, Larson recalls.

The cook detail arrived at Clark Field ahead of the other prisoners to set up kitchen service. In charge was an American prisoner named Sgt. John Shadoan, who later became Larson's good friend.

"The Japanese had given him a pig. Of course, it was rancid! You could smell that spoiled pig almost from Clark Field to Camp O'Donnell, I'll swear. Whew! That pig was ripe and full of maggots. Our cooks boiled it in this big vat filled with water, and the maggots floated to the top.

"Well, we ate that pig—maggots and all! The bugs were cooked and they were protein, so we ate them. Believe me, it was the best food we had since before the war! In all, the chow wasn't good at Clark Field either, but it wasn't any worse than what we'd had before. In fact, it was sometimes better than what we were fed on Bataan before the surrender."

Still, the prisoners were hardly getting their fill. Even when the Japanese let the POWs splurge on rice and a rancid pig, "one pig for about 200 men doesn't go very far, and everybody got just a little piece."

On fuller stomachs than they'd had in weeks, the prisoners set about organizing their new home and themselves. By the third day, the American officers were organizing POWs into platoon-sized work details for the Japanese.

Larson's group had two captains (one a medical officer) and two first lieutenants. As a staff sergeant — one of the higher-ranking noncoms (noncommissioned officers) in the larger POW group — Larson was given charge of a work platoon.

"I was responsible for three barracks. The only benefit I received from this position was extra work for myself!" Larson never lightened those extra duties, however. "Even when I was sick, I didn't stop working. And I could have stayed out, taken myself out, because I was in charge of the work assignments. I could have taken an easier job too. But, I refused to give up, and I'd try to take the rougher assignments and give the weaker guys the so-called light detail."

Each night, the Japanese would detail the next day's work to the American officers who would then communicate to platoon leaders, like Larson, how many men were needed and how much work they would have to do.

The prisoners' first assignments involved cleanup and camp security, Larson notes.

"We picked up and got rid of all the junk, which took us about a year. If we could use anything, we were allowed to bring it back to camp. We did manage to scrounge up some medical supplies such as bandages and iodine, but no quinine (for the malaria that ran rampant through the camp thanks to the area's infestation of mosquitoes)."

After the air base was shipshape, the prisoners were assigned to dig quarry rock for the airfield's runways, a grueling task to be performed by sick and exhausted men on the energy afforded them by two cups of steamed rice and some water each day.

Rocks were laboriously dug out of the ground in squads of eight to ten men, with platoon leader Larson in charge of who went where and what each man's task was. Only a visible physical injury, malaria or dengue fever would excuse a man from duty. And, as the officer in charge, Larson was never completely excused. "Even if I was sick, I still had to make my work lists and meet my quotas."

Each squad had a quota for the amount of rock its prisoners had to dig with shovels and picks each day, all day. And, the squads worked seven days a week, year round at different locations as work teams moved to find the rocks they needed. "There were no holidays, no Sundays, just work days."

And, some days were easier than others.

"If you were lucky, you found a place where you could get lots of rocks and had your quota by 4 p.m. If you were unlucky, you stayed out there sometimes until midnight looking for rocks. I'll tell you, we stayed out close to midnight several times to get our quota."

Regardless of the location or ease of extraction, the

This sketch, titled "Rules and Regulations," depicts the prisoners' welcome to their new work camp home. Sketch courtesy of Ben Steele.

quotas had to be met. After all, the Japanese had a master plan for the prisoners and, as on the Death March, the plan could not be changed.

"Someone from their engineering department had figured out that you had to get so much rock and pile it a certain way. Each pile was so long, so high, and so wide, and each pile had to meet those dimensions. It didn't matter what size rock you collected to make the pile; the predetermined pile size was what mattered. You stayed and worked until the piles were right and the quota met, sometimes all day and most of the night."

One day Larson's Japanese "foreman" either deliberately or stupidly misinterpreted the plan's design.

"This stupid Jap tried to make us build the pile straight up instead of tapering it like we were supposed to. We built it up high and then he walked on it! Well, the rocks tumbled down across my legs, and injured both my knees so badly that they had to carry me into camp. We had nothing to treat my legs with. They just had to heal as they were, and it was painful. In fact, my knees never completely healed correctly and gave me trouble for years. I finally ended up getting both knees replaced."

The rock pile was the least of Larson's concerns, however. As the man in charge of his squad and platoon, the Japanese held him responsible — and punished him — for any platoon member's infraction.

Most severe were the punishments that came when two prisoners escaped from Larson's platoon about six months apart.

"Those were two times that I really thought I was done for. The first man was engaged to a Filipino woman. He had been sick and so I assigned him to light kitchen duty. His girlfriend had taken a job at the camp kitchen after the Japanese had relaxed the rules a little and allowed local people to do the dirty work at the camp. The POW's girlfriend made contact with him in the kitchen, and they most probably made their escape plans then. He took off in the middle of the night."

The second man to escape, Taylor, was married to a Filipino woman who also worked at the camp kitchen. Taylor escaped from a work detail both he and Larson were on most likely thanks to escape plans hatched in the kitchen where his wife worked. Larson later learned that Taylor — who was just a private first class at the time of his capture — organized and ran an effective resistance group that provided valuable information, via covert communiqués, to American warships.

Larson saw neither man escape, nor did he know that their escapes were imminent. But the Japanese cared little what Larson knew. All that mattered was that he was in charge and, therefore, must be held responsible for the escapes.

"After the first escape was discovered, the Japanese raised all kinds of heck with us. First, we all had to stand in formation in the hot sun for hours, one of their favorite torture treatments."

They had another favorite torture test especially designed for the Americans they held responsible for the escapes.

"After standing in the hot sun for hours, everyone went to work except me; I went in the box — a little tin shack the Japanese put you in for days that was designed to be *very* uncomfortable.

"It was a small cubicle made of sheet metal with no openings in it except a door. The door was a piece of sheet metal with hinges that would open up, shut, and lock. They built it so you couldn't stand up and you couldn't lay down straight out. You had to curl up or squat. The building sat right out in the sun. It was made of sheet metal and got very hot during the day, but it also got surprisingly cold at night."

In the grand scheme of torture, the first day 'wasn't too bad,' Larson says. But after a night and another day, another night, and another day, it was all Larson could do to keep from giving up.

"After the first day, my mind was blank and I completely lost track of time. It was totally dark in there, and there were mosquitoes galore! I just kept praying, 'God get me through this; let me get out of here.' I couldn't sit up straight. I had no food or water. The Japanese were really masters of torture."

As hard as the box was during his three-day ordeal, Larson was able to walk away from his first experience alive and not too worse for the wear.

However, the same torture was past bearing six months later when the second man from Larson's platoon escaped, this time from an airfield detail.

"During assembly after work, the Japanese discovered Taylor was missing. They marched us in front of the camp headquarters building, surrounded us with guards, and kept us standing until about 4 a.m. We didn't know what was going to happen, and I thought they were getting ready to shoot us all.

"The next morning, they turned us loose, but later that day after everyone had gone to work, they called the officers and myself to Japanese headquarters. A regular detail of Japanese guards escorted our camp commander Captain Fleming (sic), our medical officer and myself there.

"On the way, we thought we were going to be shot. In fact, Captain Fleming said, 'Let's die like men and show them we can die like men.' When we arrived, they didn't get physical or shoot us. We were grilled for about two hours through an interpreter. They asked about the man, did we know where he was going, how come he left, etc. Heck, we had no idea he was going to escape! The two soldiers involved never talked to us or said they were going over the hill. When they realized we didn't know anything, they turned us loose. That was the most frightening time of my entire captivity!"

What happened next proved one of the most physically and emotionally challenging times of Larson's POW experience.

"To punish me for not knowing or not stopping the escape, I went back in the box. This time for seven days! No food, no water, just me in the box."

It was a level of torture that Larson insists he never would have endured without his faith and a Good Samaritan hidden within the Japanese ranks.

"There was one Japanese soldier who must have had the lowest rank. He always got the midnight shift guarding that shack. And, as he had during my first confinement, he would slip me a canteen and, every once in a

These old storage buildings are among the few standing reminders of the Clark Field Concentration Camp that stood here in World War II. Photo by Rick Peterson.

while, a rice ball. It didn't happen every night because I don't know how often he was on duty. Each time he slipped me something, he made signs to make sure I didn't tell anybody.

"The second time in the box, I am sure that I would have died without his help," Larson admits, adding that even with the undercover provisions, he still had to be carried from the shack.

"I couldn't walk out. They had to carry me back to the barracks and put me in my bunk. But the Japanese left me alone after that, and I was able to rest for a couple of days before I had to go back to work."

Perhaps because Larson had been the one directly in charge of the escapee work group — or for whatever torturous whim — the Japanese spared the other officers involved from "the box," and the American officers who marched to the Japanese hut that day lived long enough to enjoy their country's victory and their liberation.

To ensure there would be no more escapes, the Japanese came up with a convincing prevention technique. They formed prisoners into groups of ten called "death squads."

"These groups consisted of the ten men that slept next to each other. We all knew that if any one of the squad escaped, the other nine men would be shot and killed. We had no more escapes after that because you knew that your escape would condemn your buddies to death."

Larson is sure that no prisoners escaped after the death squads were formed because the whole camp would have been made painfully aware of the consequences.

Besides killing the escapee's death squad members, the escapees would have been brought to the camp to be publicly tortured and killed, Larson insists.

"That's why I know they never caught the two escapees because they would have made us see what such an act would bring us."

Public punishment for any infraction was a familiar lesson for the POWs.

"The Japanese wanted everyone to know they meant business. For example, prior to the death squad formations, the Japanese had caught two Filipinos stealing corrugated sheet metal from some storage buildings. The Japanese made us fall out and stand in formation. They brought the Filipinos in front us, tied each one to a post, and used them for bayonet practice until they were dead. We had to stand in formation and watch the whole thing."

Most often, the Grim Reaper arrived in the forms of illness and hopelessness.

"We didn't have any medical supplies for anything. We had no quinine for malaria and nothing to treat anything with whatsoever. If you got hurt or sick you pretty much just suffered and either made it or died."

If someone was really bad off medically, the medical officer could send him to the Japanese hospital. "In the Philippines, one soldier with a bad case of appendicitis was sent to their hospital and our doctor couldn't go with him. He came back to us in worse shape than when he left because they cut him up so badly that he was physically ruined for the rest of his life. He was cut from shoulder to hip, and I think they experimented on him.

"The Japanese didn't use anesthetic when they operated on prisoners, and we didn't have anesthetic either, of course. If we had a tooth problem, the medical officer would pull them with a pair of pliers. Basically, if you had something that needed operating, you just had to bear it. For example, one POW — who was not in our camp and had been captured on Wake Island — had to have his appendix out. His own corpsman operated on him. For anesthetic, seven marines held him down."

The Japanese had little sympathy for most prisoners' maladies, though they did recognize malaria and actual physical injuries (like a broken arm) and would not make a POW work. "The Japanese would come out and check when you reported sick. If they saw malaria, there was no question in their minds about that because they were also afflicted with it. If you got hurt, and they could see you were hurt, they didn't make you work. But, they would come and check on you every single day. The second you looked better, it was back to work for you."

Larson suffered through bouts with malaria at Clark Field and still remembers the hot and cold roller coaster the disease inflicted on its victims.

"You could feel malaria coming on, no question about it. You would get so hot that everything would come off and you were still hot. You sweat like a dog. Malaria would make you want to take your skin off! The next minute you would shake and shiver and feel like you were freezing to death. You couldn't get enough covers on you. I had recurring bouts of malaria, even after we returned to America, though they gradually became further and further apart."

Yet, for some unknown reason or twist of fate, Larson was spared other excruciating, embarrassing and exhausting illnesses that plagued and killed other POWs by the thousands.

"There were several kinds of fever. Dengue fever and malaria were the bad ones, and from the sufferer's point of view they're basically the same because you get the chills and the sweats with both of them. I had dengue fever in the Philippines before the war and hoped I'd suffer nothing like that again. Then I got malaria as a POW and found out that it could be worse than I thought."

While dysentery (severe and painful, often bloody, diarrhea) and malaria remained the most persistent prison maladies, most prisoners would also suffer outbreaks of beriberi, a disease caused by severe vitamin deficiency.

"Because of our diet, every prisoner I knew had dengue fever, malaria and beriberi at one time or another. Beriberi is a vitamin B deficiency disease that we got because of our diet — or lack of diet — especially because the rice we were served was polished, meaning all the nutrients had been taken out of it. The result was that our veins would fill with fluid and swell up, leaving a big dent (where the swelling was)."

"I got beriberi too and swelled up around the legs and ankles, but some guys got it so bad that it was called elephantiasis and their scrotum and testicles would swell up huge. Because we had no medical supplies whatsoever to treat them and no vitamins to improve their condition, all they could do was soak in cold water and try to bring the swelling down."

Many times the swelling would move up the body, through the organs and to the heart, a fatal progression. To try to stem the swelling and stop the illness, doctors would cut a slit in a POWs stomach to relieve the pressure, according to *The Bataan Death March: A Collaborative Project.*

The nutritional supplements needed to fight and prevent diseases rarely found their way into the POWs' daily water and rice diet. What supplements arrived relied equally on hard work, luck, ingenuity, and Filipino — and even Japanese — "generosity."

For example, the POWs occasionally got salt to put on their food and were sometimes given soybeans and other greens from the fields. "We could cook them in hot water. They were hard but nutritious and we ate them. But, we could never soften those danged things up. Still, when they were cooked, at least you could chew them."

Once, the Japanese even let the POW workers pool their ten-cents-a-day wages (paid in worthless Japanese scrip) to buy a carabao from the nearby Filipino village for meat.

"The Japanese went and got it from the Filipinos, brought it in the camp, and we killed it. We dug a big pit and filled it full of rocks. We built a fire so the rocks got real hot, put the carabao in the pit, and covered it up with rocks and grass. We let it cook for a couple of days and then we dug it up. Boy, was that tender meat!"

It was a small taste treat shared by about 200 men.

Other delicacies had to be stolen or captured. Dietary supplements included snakes, rats, and occasional birds that had the misfortune of landing too close to a hungry but fast POW.

"Other than my injury from the rocks, the bayoneting of the thieving Filipinos, the two escape episodes, spending time in the shack, thinking I was going to be shot two different times, and the diseases we were subject to, life in camp was pretty routine."

"Especially when we were working, an animal might wander through the work area. If it was big enough, such as a snake or the like, we would kill it and bring it back for the cooks to prepare so that everyone could share it. If it was a small animal or just a vegetable or something, the person would keep it for himself and fix it as his personal 'quan' (a name given to anything a prisoner cooked or prepared for his own use). There was no hoarding food; it was eaten as soon as it was available.

"In camp, the prisoners would set up traps to catch small rodents so they would have something to quan for extra food. Everybody had his own quan bucket to prepare whatever he caught. There were a few men who would not eat snake or rats or any of the other delicacies that wandered through camp. These men usually did not survive imprisonment."

Though food and survival remained the primary focus of each POW day, Larson says POWs fell into a sort of drudging daily schedule.

"Other than my injury from the rocks, the bayoneting of the thieving Filipinos, the two escape episodes, spending time in the shack, thinking I was going to be shot two different times, and the diseases we were subject to, life in camp was pretty routine."

Seven days a week, 365 days a year, the POWs at Clark Field toiled for the Japanese. There were no holidays, no Sundays, and by and large no sick days.

Most days, when rock quotas were filled, the POWs

labored from sunrise until about 6 p.m. when the evening cup of rice was served.

On those days, the prisoners might find some evening moments to talk with each other, read one of a few English books or newspapers the Filipinos were able to smuggle them, or think of anything but their predicament or, worse, home.

"We were always too damned tired to do much. We got up, worked, ate our meals, and went to bed. We never celebrated holidays; they were just like any other day. We knew when the holidays were, of course, but we didn't discuss them. At Christmas, I think everyone thought about it, as I did, but in our situation thinking about what holidays used to be or should be was too painful. You couldn't let your mind go there too much."

Some prisoners made instruments, or sang, or occasionally performed for the camp to keep up morale. Among them was Larson who, somewhere along the way, had found a harmonica to help bide his time. He also had played the guitar before the war and would pluck on a guitar that a fellow prisoner had made and tuned into the key of C using Larson's harmonica.

Such entertainment nearly got Larson in serious trouble one night.

"One time I was lying in the barracks and, just for kicks, I rhythmically played one note over and over. A Japanese unit came storming in with bayonets fixed and demanded to know where the radio was! They thought I was sending a code. Well, I showed them what I was doing and that, fortunately, was the end of that."

Very occasionally, Larson would pass the time writing letters home in the dim hope that the Japanese might actually mail them and his family might know that their son was alive.

"I don't remember how many letters I wrote but it

was more than one. Shortly before leaving Clark Field in June 1944, everyone received a standard, prewritten card with English messages that we could check. For example, one was 'I am well.' Another was 'I am sick.' After we checked a message, we would sign the card; we were not allowed to write anything on it but our signature. We were darn sure if we checked anything but 'I am well' the card would never get out. We wondered if any of our mail got out of camp! The only reason we filled them out was to try and let people back home know we were still alive. Later on, we were not able to send and receive any kind of mail from Japan."

Larson's hunches were right. The cards were never mailed. Word of them did, however, travel all the way back to Minnesota.

"Instead of mailing them, the Japanese would get on a radio, say a POW's name, and repeat the checked message, 'I am well.' I found out after the war that two or three HAM radio operators in San Francisco, California, intercepted the Japanese messages. They forwarded them to my mother, Hilda. The HAM operators all had the same message coming from different sources. Consequently, my mother and family knew I was alive."

The family didn't hear from Larson again for more than a year, however, and doubts of his safety began to creep in.

From his side of the Pacific, Larson knew little more about his family than they did about him. A few V-mail letters with twenty-five words or less from his mother did get through to him at Clark Field after his capture as well as some short, typed letters.

In addition to a few letters, Larson did get one Red Cross package while he was still in the Philippines.

"The Japanese guards had opened it up and taken items out. They were especially after cigarettes. We got a can of powdered milk and one of condensed milk. It was real thick and sugary. There was coffee, tea, and a tin container with meat in it. That was about it. Some people sat down and ate everything right away. Boy, did they get sick.

"Worse were the prisoners who traded their food for what cigarettes were left in the packages. They would rather have the cigarettes than food; most of them didn't survive."

The only other packages the POWs enjoyed were the English newspapers and materials that Filipino workers would smuggle to prisoners when they were together on work details.

"Filipinos worked up in the Japanese kitchen every day besides working in ours and they were in other details in the hangars; in the fields hauling things, quarrying rocks, or whatever the Japanese wanted done. While they were there, the Filipinos would carefully give us information about the war's progress or newspapers (which the Japanese printed in English because the Philippines was an American territory and many Filipinos spoke English) that we could read for ourselves. The papers would never say that the Japanese were retreating. They were always 'advancing to prepared positions in the rear.'"

By the spring of 1944, such notices provided the prisoners a growing number of clues that the tide of war was turning and that America and her allies were pushing the Japanese back.

"We knew things were going bad for the Japanese because we saw that a lot of the 'old timers' among the Japanese guards were leaving, most probably because they were needed on the line. At the same time, we were getting 'conscript' soldiers from Korea to take their place."

In June 1944, the POWs watched as the Japanese

started to prepare to ship out of the Philippines. "We knew darned well then that the Americans were getting close. And the Filipinos would occasionally tell us, 'Don't worry, Joe. War over soon.'"

The Japanese instructed the prisoner officers to select a small cadre of about fifty men who would stay behind to dismantle the camp. "Though they were promised transfer to a new camp, the Japanese executed these remaining prisoners before shipping out themselves. We learned about this after the war from Filipinos who remained at Clark Field and survived."

By the end of June 1944, Clark Field was dismantled as a concentration camp and its prisoners, including Larson, were traveling sixty miles in American-made trucks to the port of Manila, where they would be shipped to new working assignments in Japan.

"We didn't know what to expect about going into the Lion's Den so to speak. Everyone at least hoped that Japan couldn't or wouldn't be worse than the Philippines, even though we probably had it the best of any prison camp in the Philippines when we were at Clark Field.

"We didn't talk about being executed; in fact, that never entered my mind. We only found out about Japanese mass executions and their plans for mass executions after the war." (In fact, in one mass execution case on Palawan, the Japanese ordered remaining POWs into a trench, soaked the prisoners in gasoline and lit the trench on fire, shooting any prisoners who tried to escape.)

The Clark Field prisoners were first transported to Bilibid Prison, a former penal institution in Manila and much used Japanese prisoner transfer point. They arrived, and left, wearing the same uniforms they had been captured in more than two years before—a pair of khaki pants, a khaki shirt, and underwear.

"Bilibid was the most boring place you ever saw. We just sat around the whole time. There were no facilities and no work because we were going to ship out. As soon as we woke up in the morning, the guards mustered us outside. We weren't confined to a cell though. There was a common bathroom for everyone to use, about 10 commodes in all for my area. Of the 1,162 prisoners there, about 300 were from Clark Field at that time. Most everybody just wandered around the compound, which was one big open courtyard, and everyone slept in buildings on concrete floors. We just sat around the whole time."

But, monotony and boredom are their own forms of torture.

"Time didn't really mean anything at Bilibid. I'm not even sure what time they fed us, and that was an important time because we always kept track of food. I just lived from day to day and didn't project myself any further. If anyone had stayed there very long, they would have gone stark raving nuts!"

By August 1944, the prisoners were more than ready to leave the monotonous existence they endured at Bilibid. Little did they know they would soon be willing to sell their souls to return to that "paradise."

RIDING THROUGH HELL ON WATER

On August 9, 1944, some 1,162 Bilibid prisoners were crammed into the forward hold of an inter-island Japanese freighter called the Noto Maru in Manila harbor for what would normally be a few days' ride to Japan.

The trip lasted twenty-three days, or twenty-three lifetimes by the prisoners' count.

Larson's experience began August 9 but did not get under way until several days later, he recalls.

"They took us by ferries to the middle of the harbor where the Noto Maru was the only ship loading American prisoners in a harbor that was quite congested with ships. We boarded the Noto Maru by walking up a big old gangplank."

The Noto Maru was one of several Japanese ships that attempted to carry prisoners of war to Japan. The cramped, rancid, air-starved, half-mad conditions in the hulls of ships, into which thousands of men were stuffed, earned the Noto Maru and POW transport ships like it the nickname of Hell Ships.

After the Bataan Death March, the bulk of POW deaths at the hands of the Japanese occurred aboard the Hell Ships.

Some 5,000 POWs died on the ships. Hundreds perished from the conditions on board and thousands from American attacks. For example in late 1944, nearly 700 POWs on board the Shinyo Maru and nearly 286 on board the Oryoku Maru died when these transport ships were sunk by U.S. Navy attacks, according to the report "Americans Know Very Little About The Hell Ships of World War II" written by Ruth E. Jorgenson. Sadly, she adds, five hundred of the Oryoku Maru survivors were later killed when a U.S. Navy bomber sunk their replacement ship, Enoura Maru. Most horrifically, only eight of the 1,800 POWs on board the Arisan Maru survived when it was torpedoed and sunk in October 1944.

Larson's own perilous journey began when "the Japanese ran us down into the ship's hot 1,000-square-foot hold. It was in the middle of the day, and it was already hotter than Billy Blazes before we added our 1,162 men into it. When we were loaded in the hold, they hauled up the ladder. There was no way to get out of that place or communicate well with anyone. The hatch in the hold was the only fresh air and light we had."

The men were divided into five companies with a prisoner officer in charge of each, and each company was assigned to enter a different section of the hold. Company One was the first to board and went way back in the hold. Company Two boarded a little bit closer to the opening, Company Three got closer yet, Company Four closer yet, and Company Five was right in front. Larson was in Company Four, which was, luckily, relatively close to the hatch.

Just getting under way was nearly as unbearable as the conditions they were about to get under way in, Larson recalls.

"We went through boarding and disembarking three times before we finally sailed. We would go there, get on the ship, get in the hold, and the next day they would take us all off. I don't know why. There probably was submarines around or some reason not to sail. We finally boarded for good on August 13 but still waited in the hold two days before we sailed. We left Manila Harbor on August 15, 1944."

The cruising accommodations were inhuman at best.

"It was not a luxury cruise by any means; cattle had better accommodations. There was not enough space to stretch out. You had to sit with your knees pulled in front of you and lean on the knees of the person behind you and the back of the person in front of you. For toilet facilities we had a large wooden bucket that the Japanese would hoist up and dump overboard when it became full.

"The latrine was a big tub about six feet across and about three feet deep. It was located directly below the opening above on deck. To get there you had to crawl over everyone. When you did, you lost your place. In addition, the Japanese were not too careful when they raised the tub and some of the contents would spill down on some of the prisoners.

"In addition, some people were sick. They stayed in the very front of the hold where the 'Benjo Bucket' (latrine) was. They could lie down there while the rest of us either stood or squatted and tried to be comfortable.

"Since I was in Company Four and next to the last to get down into the hold, it wasn't so bad for me because I was close to the middle of the hold. The hatch was open but didn't provide much ventilation even though we were closer to it. Needless to say, it reeked and it was hot!

"There wasn't any light at all either so you did most of your eating, maneuvering and relieving in the dark. During the day, the hatch was open, but it was still dark most of the time. Even if the hatch was open at night, that didn't change anything because in the tropics, nighttime is like pulling a shade over everything. There is nothing blacker than a tropical sky at night!"

To make matters worse for the overheated, hungry and sick men, the ship's prisoners were kept starving.

"We were fed (if you were lucky enough to get some) once a day. Water was rationed out, and here again, you were lucky if you got some. Like food, the Japanese sent water down once a day in a big old bucket. If you didn't get any maybe a friend would give you some if he got it. He would if he got some, and I got a cup every once in a while. We were fortunate if we got one cup of water and one cup of rice a day. It was hell!"

Despite the torturous accommodations, the men on Larson's Hell Ship didn't take their maddening situation out on each other.

"Surprisingly, after we got settled in, there was very little fighting. Tempers would flare once in a while, but that was short lived. Everybody was in the absolute same 'boat' as everyone else."

The Noto Maru first sailed through the China Sea to Takao, a port at Formosa, and it did not sail alone.

"We knew there were more ships in the convoy, but had no idea how many. Some soldiers were able to get up on deck by faking sickness and could see other ships. We went to China and took so long to get to Japan because we zigzagged back and forth to avoid American submarines."

The first day in Formosa the prisoners were hurried above decks for a quick wash down before returning to their dank and darkened hell below the water line. It was the one and only respite for most, Larson recalls.

"When we got on deck, they sprayed us down with ice-cold salt water from pressure hoses. After about ten minutes, they ran us down into the hold. We sat there in that dark, smelly hold after that and never left our hole again until we reached Japan."

The next day, the prisoners cheered and feared a welcome sign that the Allies were advancing, and fast, against the Japanese.

"We could hear planes (American B-17s) coming and didn't know they were bombers until the bombs started falling. I guess the attack lasted about 45 minutes and I don't think they hit much in the harbor. Thankfully for us as prisoners anyway, their aim was atrocious."

The B-17s had no way to know they were bombing American prisoners. "The Japanese didn't mark their ships with Red Crosses or any markings whatsoever! Besides prisoners, our ship carried Japanese troops, civilians, and who knows what else."

The day after the bombing, the Hell Ship headed back out to sea and toward the lurking dangers of submarine torpedoes.

On their ever-turning route toward Japan, the convoy and the Noto Maru came under Allied submarine attack.

"We knew something was happening because the Japanese brandished the machine gun they had on deck at us. It was like they were saying, 'You better not try and come up!'

"At first our hatch was open and we could see the Japanese running around up on deck very excited. They pulled our rope ladder out of the hold, and we started to hear and feel a lot of 'thuds,' which were exploding depth charges."

Despite the threat of being blown from the water, the prisoners were more hopeful that the sub would damage the Japanese than worried that they would be hurt.

"I would say ninety-nine percent of us were calm

"If I would have been in that hold much longer, I probably would have gone insane!"

during the attack. I was thinking, and many people were actually saying, 'Hit us! Hit us!'

"We soon heard and felt one tremendous explosion and saw a big glare in the sky. This had to have happened when a Japanese tanker was hit. Since we were in the hold, we couldn't see any actual fire. We all got excited and when we saw the glare, everybody hollered, 'Yeah!' Right after that, the Japanese closed the hatch so we couldn't see anything."

The Noto Maru escaped the submarine.

"We continued to zigzag, and the submarines chased us for quite a while. I don't know if any other ships were hit. But after the attack was over, they peeled off the hatch. Shortly after that, it was daylight, so we figured the attack had lasted several hours."

Even after the attack the Japanese were wary of their prisoner cargo and kept a machine gun pointed their direction.

After twenty-three days in that "awful hot and stinking hold," Larson's Hell Ship beat the odds and survived the passage — as did Larson and most of the prisoners on board.

"Though Company Four had no deaths on the ship, there were some that died en route, those that were in the positions farthest away from the hatch, in Companies 1 and 2. They had it the worst because they were so far from the food and water distribution that they were lucky to get fed once a week. I seem to remember some burials at sea where they pulled the dead out and tossed them overboard, but my memories of the Hell Ship are mostly blocked. I don't remember much of anything past the first few days."

When the Noto Maru pulled into port at Moji, Japan, on September 6, 1944, Larson was assigned to a detail that allowed him on deck.

"I don't remember what the detail was, but they put the ladder down and I went up on deck. I was in the first small group to climb out of that hold. When I got on deck, I knew my name, rank, and serial number, and that was all I knew! If I would have been in that hold much longer, I probably would have gone insane!"

Rides much longer than Larson's did drive men insane, he adds. For as bad as their ride aboard the Noto Maru was, Larson soon heard how much worse it could have been.

Another ship, which left the same day as Larson's, reportedly took forty-five days to arrive because it had to spend a great deal of time dodging American submarines and ships. The extended time in Hell Ship conditions reportedly turned prisoners against each other.

"Some prisoners on other ships like that one turned into vampires," a horror confirmed by a friend Larson got reacquainted with after they'd been freed and were awaiting shipment home. "A mutual friend of ours went wild on that ship and started trying to drink people's blood to quench his own thirst. Gonzalez was practically crying then as he told me how he and others had to beat our friend to death with their hands.

"I heard that similar things happened on other ships. One officer had to reportedly help kill his own son because he had become a vampire. I'm not sure if it's true but having been on one of those ships, I'd believe it. We were all so close to going insane in those conditions."

Prisoner John M. Wright Jr. endured such insane conditions on board the Oryoku Maru in December 1944. In his book *Capture on Corregidor*, Wright notes how he bore witness to the vampire-style attacks and insanity-driven murders that Larson had only feared.

"A blood curdling scream pierced the blackness and confusion," he writes. "The first man to commit suicide had slashed his wrists with a razor ... Soon there were more screams with shouted threats and violent swearing. ... Several men went raving mad and charged through the mob swinging knives and empty canteens. The yelling of the men who were attacked added to the bedlam. ...We all had to defend ourselves from possible assaults. That led to the assumption that any man who bumped into another might be an attacker and the best defense was to get him before he got you. A number of men undoubtedly were murdered when they inadvertently bumped into someone. ... Several human vampires fought their way through the panic stricken mob, biting men and sucking blood in their mad thirst for liquid. Some others sucked the blood from warm corpses.

"I believe that it was the basic innate, mental, moral and physical stamina that flowed in a man's veins since his babyhood that enabled him to come through that night sanely," Wright adds.

WORKING FOR 'THE HOMELAND'

Though Larson and the surviving POWs of the Noto Maru were relieved to be off the Hell Ship when they disembarked in Japan, they remained apprehensive about what the Japanese had in store for them next as they herded the men by company onto a ferry and then into a big warehouse across the bay in Shimonoseki, Japan.

"The guards stripped us down, took away our old clothes, and gave us Japanese military uniforms. We got clean clothes but didn't get to wash and clean up. We didn't get anything to eat until we got to the warehouse where we got a big rice ball, a slice of apple, a piece of fish, and water to drink. It was the best food we had in years!"

After an overnight stay in the warehouse, the POWs were awakened before dawn to board a passenger train for a ride to their next work stations.

"The Japanese made us pull the window shades clear down because they didn't want civilians to see us. They said the civilians would riot and cause us harm if they saw us, but I find this doubtful now because the civilians we knew in Japan weren't that way. The civilians we knew in Japan treated us real well; it was the military we had problems with."

Larson's second train ride as a POW was far more

tolerable than his first. Not only did he have a reasonably comfortable place to sit, there was fresh air and a substantial meal, by POW standards anyway.

"When we boarded the train, we were given a box lunch. It contained a big rice ball, a cucumber, and an apple. The train didn't travel very fast and stopped often to let off prisoners at work sites the Japanese had selected in advance. Since I was in Company Four, we were the next to the last group to disembark."

The last two groups traveled to their final POW destinations via Tokyo with Company Five continuing on the train to a coal mining town in northern Japan called Hanawa while Larson's Company Four changed trains and headed due west out of Tokyo for a day and a half.

"We passed through the town of Takaoka, which had a big steel mill. The town was about fifteen or twenty miles southwest of our future camp, Camp Namachi."

The camp was set in the Japanese flatlands and was surrounded by villages and open fields that the prisoners could see. The view may have been picturesque but the climate was far less welcoming.

"The summer was hotter than Hades, and the winter was as cold as Minnesota, except we weren't dressed for it. At our camp, however, we were lucky because we got two blankets each so, when we got done working, we could climb under the blankets and stay warm.

"In the wintertime, I ate supper out of my mess kit on my bed and then I crawled right in because it was very cold and snowed like you wouldn't believe. The snowfall was heavy, but we never had a snow day off of work. The civilians would shovel a path to the machine shop and the dock. I don't know how, but it was always open after a snowfall. There was nothing to shovel the camp compound with, so we just packed the snow down when we walked on it.

"We were issued a jacket for winter, along with hob-nailed boots. Other than that, we wore Japanese military uniforms with baggy pants, and we were cold."

That cold, snowy place proved to be Larson's home for the next year — a year the POW has since described as his "dead year" — a monotonous time when he got no outside information, had nothing to read or do and spent every day all day working, tired and hungry.

"This camp had been prepared for us and was ready and waiting to house a large number of POWs, unlike Camp O'Donnell from so long ago. There were two large barracks with toilet facilities, running water, and a mess hall. The barracks offered us two tiers of bunks with big straw mattresses that were harder than bricks! Each prisoner was also issued blankets and a neck-breaking, hard pillow. There were several strands of barbed wire fence about ten feet high around the camp and some guards, but that was all they had to keep us in. Again, there was little thought of escape because where could we go that someone wouldn't spot us as Americans, especially in Japan?"

The POWs were given no time to adjust to their new surroundings and went to work immediately the next morning. "We acclimated as we worked and learned what that work would be through an interpreter who relayed the camp officer's orders to our officers who then dispersed the orders to us accordingly."

The camp officer giving the POWs their orders was nicknamed The One-Armed Bandit by the prisoners because he had lost an arm fighting in China. As camp commanders went, The One-Armed Bandit was tolerable. "As long as you did your work, he left you alone. He wasn't a bad guy. He never beat or physically abused anybody that I saw, which many Japanese camp commanders did — and brutally — at other camps.

For example, in *The Janesville 99* by Zarette R. Beard,

Alf Larson was given this rare photo taken of himself, (ninth from right, back row) other prisoners and guards including the One-Armed Bandit, shortly after Japan's surrender.

Private Guiles reports that among witnessing such torture treatments as pulling out prisoners' finger and toenails, he survived one of the most horrifying Japanese torture tactics used more commonly at other camps and in interrogations, known as the water treatment. "They took a water hose and stuck it down my throat and turned (the water) on. Believe it or not, your stomach swells to where you look pregnant. Then, they put their boot on my stomach and it was just like a geyser…. I was lucky to survive that because in most cases it resulted in death."

The One-Armed Bandit rarely used such tactics on his prisoners, Larson reports. He did, however, like his Saki, and often confused prisoners with unusual, drunken requests.

"For example, each week in the wintertime, he saw that we were issued a couple of pieces of wood for heat. We had one pot-bellied stove right in the middle of the barracks, which was supposed to heat the whole place but never did. When he drank, he would have Saki in his head and come 'roaring drunk' into our barracks. He'd tell us to 'fire the stove up, get it hot! I'll get you more wood tomorrow.' Well, we fired it up but never got any additional wood. He promised, but I don't think he had the wood to give us. I had no idea why he came in!"

By and large, other Japanese guards — military and civilian — left the working POWs alone. "They came, did their shifts, and left. There were fewer beatings and torture like we saw in the Philippines, at least at Camp Namachi."

There was still plenty of hard, long work and little food to sustain a working man.

"We always got up early and generally worked ten to twelve hours a day. Our alarm clocks were the military guards. They would come in the barracks early every morning, holler, and stomp their feet. That woke everybody up! We got up and got dressed. Then we would have a bowl of lugao, that soupy rice. Each morning, after we'd eaten, a civilian guard would escort us to our detail. We were escorted back to camp for lunch, which was a cooked rice ball, and then back to work. We'd eat more soupy rice — which was thinner than cream of wheat or oatmeal — for supper, and I would get about a canteen cup of that 'goulash.' Occasionally we'd get soybeans or fish to supplement our diet, and we got this more often than we had in the Philippines, but it still wasn't enough to keep us healthy.

"After supper, no one felt like doing anything. We didn't have anything to talk about or anything to read. We never had any cards to play or any cigarettes to smoke. There were absolutely no facilities there for us, or anything to do! We'd just go to bed. It was quiet in the barracks; you could hear a mouse walk in there — and if you actually did hear a mouse you'd heave a shoe at him and try to catch and eat him. The camp rule was whoever caught the rat got to eat him."

If Larson did anything between working, eating and sleeping, it was reading the Bible that he managed to sneak through the Death March, the Philippines and into Japan. "I read it every day and prayed by myself every day. In Japan I didn't worry about the guards seeing it and taking it away because we never had shakedowns there like we did in the Philippines. If they'd found it at Clark Field, they would have taken it."

The Good Book was Larson's only refuge from the monotonous toiling of the work camp. "The work itself wasn't that demanding, but we were strapped by the end of the day because the work we were doing was being done on so few calories. Surviving on starvation rations resulted in a very low strength and tolerance level. So, most of the time, when I was done with work, I just 'zonked out.'"

Sleep was never entirely peaceful at Camp Namachi, Larson recalls. "There were bed lice in the straw mattresses and blankets. We'd wake up every morning with bites all over our bodies. We had no medication or means to get rid of them so we just had to get used to it. People might find this hard to believe, but we did get used to it and didn't really notice the lice after a while."

While most prisoners worked in smelting operations across the bay, Larson and another prisoner, Floyd Wade, were fortunate enough to be assigned machine shop duty about a half-mile from camp.

"The Japanese had come through and asked our commander if anyone could run a lathe. There were two of us who knew how to operate one. They took us to a machine shop and we worked on the lathes. That's where I worked the whole time during my captivity in Japan. I was more fortunate than most people in camp."

Larson's primary work on the lathe was making wheels out of cast drums for the trolleys used in the smelting plant.

"The drums were in a rough shape. It was my job to set up the lathe to bring it down to the tolerance. Then I would bore a hole for the axle to a tolerance. The parts were all the same size. It was monotonous work but definitely better than quarrying rock! Working in the machine shop was definitely more stimulating, and I was able to think and use my mind."

The shop itself was loosely run provided that military guards weren't around. "Thankfully, they weren't around often. We had civilian guards most of the time on the machine shop detail because they didn't have enough military personnel available to guard us. The military guards we had were actually mostly armed

Korean soldiers conscripted into the Japanese army. The Japanese didn't trust the Koreans to fight for them but let them guard prisoners.

"Civilian guards were more lenient. They would never make you bow or anything and didn't slap you around or make you stand at attention, unless a military guard came around."

Larson remembers the machine shop's civilian guard fondly.

"He was the ugliest guy you ever saw. His buckteeth were something else. He could have eaten corn off the cob twenty feet away. But, he was the most good-hearted man I knew and after the surrender, he invited the two of us for dinner at his house, which was something special because the Japanese civilians didn't have much more than we did to survive on. They were just about as bad off as we were that last year of the war; the only difference was that they weren't confined."

In all, about a dozen Japanese civilians worked at the machine shop with Larson doing various tasks. The civilians were cordial to the prisoners and tried to communicate through sign language because few spoke English. "If a military guard came around, though, they'd clam up and ignore us."

There was one civilian at the shop whom Larson especially remembers.

"They gave me a 'gofer,' a young Japanese boy who brought materials and helped me. He couldn't understand English and I couldn't understand Japanese. We communicated in sign language. I would show him what I wanted and he would get it, until one time he got tangled up in my running lathe.

"To operate the lathe properly with the big castings we used big extended arms to hold them in place. Our Japanese gofer was there and he pointed to the lathe. I said, 'Oh, look out!' because he put his arm where he shouldn't have. His arm was broken so the bone was sticking out. He was in horrible pain. The other Japanese pointed and roared with laughter as if it was the funniest thing they'd seen! They didn't do a thing to help him. The other prisoner and I picked him up and carried him to the dispensary."

The only other break in the monotony came when a forceful earthquake hit the camp, Larson recalls.

"One time, at work, we had a violent earthquake. We knew what it was because we had experienced one in the Philippines. This one was worse and scarier! The Japanese were just as afraid as we were, and everyone cleared out and scattered as soon as the tremors started. There were big concrete buckets — larger than a regular washtub — outside of the shop, which contained water to fight fires with if needed. During the earthquake, the water sloshed over the tops of the tubs and telephone poles were swaying back and forth. The tremors lasted about five minutes, and when they quit, everyone came back to the shop. We could have easily escaped, but where would we have gone?"

While the POWs toiled as hard as malnutrition enabled them, all their hard work was not as it appeared to the Japanese guards, Larson stresses.

"Everybody tried to do whatever they could to sabotage things. For example, in the machine shop, we'd oversize the holes by just a little bit which would make their jobs harder to do. And, though I was an airplane mechanic and flight engineer before the surrender, I told the Japanese that I had been a clerk because I didn't want them to know I could fix their airplanes for them. You would be surprised how many clerk typists we had among the POWs!"

Meanwhile, POWs in other Japanese camps were equally resourceful and defiant. For example, hundreds of prisoners forced to build ships for Mitsubishi Corporation in Yokohama, Japan, made many subtle efforts to sabotage the ships and the material used to build them, reports former Yokohama prisoner Dave Brenzel in *The Hero Next Door® Returns*. "In any of our wanderings, it was understood that we picked up anything left unguarded. ... Where (a POW) carried it was what counted. It usually wound up in the drink or close to the bottom of the scrap pile. ... Rivets in the heating pot tended to be heated into uselessness or were not quite hot enough when needed. Air hoses and welding cables worked their way to positions where walking cranes or shifting plates would cut them," Brenzel notes, adding that even unintentional defects could be kept in the system with a little POW help. "When inspectors tested a rivet — by tapping on it — they'd circle defective rivets with white paint. The self-assumed duty of any POW in the area was to remove the circle, if he got a chance."

A handful of POWs did not join in the sabotaging efforts and even helped the Japanese fix up trucks or airplanes, in hopes, Larson supposed, of winning Japanese favor and more food and better survival chances. "In the end, this backfired on them though. Every POW shunned the Quisling turncoats that actually collaborated with the Japs, and they got little help from their fellow POWs."

Some POWs in Japan went so far the other way as to refuse to work for the Japanese at all. Though the public torture and punishment wasn't as severe or common in Japan as it had been in the Philippines, the Japanese still quickly made an example of the POWs and impressed again upon their prisoners who was in charge.

"When the Japanese found out, they put this group in a special hut outside our barracks and cut their regular food rations in half. There was no way they could make it on such few calories. They didn't work, and they didn't survive. They were starved to death!

"I don't think those guys knew the Japanese were going to starve them when they first went in there, and a few soon changed their minds and decided to work. But, it was too late. They were too far-gone. Everybody left that hut in a box. The Japanese cremated them, like they did all the prisoners who died in Japan, and put their remains in a little box. So in the end, they got what they wanted, I guess. They never did work for the Japanese again."

As with all POW deaths in Japan, the camp's highest-ranking prisoners were given the remains to guard during their captivity, and eventually take home to the prisoners' families.

The seemingly kind gesture was really the final insult, Larson notes. "We've since learned from former prisoners, like Maj. Richard M. Gordon (USA Ret.), who have been back to and talked to former Japanese officers, that the Japanese never really cremated most of our dead. They threw them in mass graves and filled the boxes with ashes from their fires. Apparently, they didn't want to waste the wood they needed for their fires on cremating dead prisoners. Even in death, they tortured us."

Though the death toll as a whole greatly diminished among the prisoners in Japan, more POWs continued to suffer and die from the effects of malnutrition than from any other malady or injury.

"Our most serious medical problem was malnutrition. We were all suffering from it in Japan even worse than in the Philippines. In the Philippines, at least, some prisoners got some food and even medicine smuggled to them through the Filipino resistance movement. Or, we could pick up weeds and stuff to eat when we went out on details, and there we ate everything that moved, grew, swam, whatever. In Japan, there was no resistance movement, and we didn't have the opportunity to scrounge for food. We had only what the Japanese gave us, and it wasn't enough.

"I was always hungry. Always! I was hungry before the American surrender on Bataan, and from the days of the Bataan Death March until we were liberated. My stomach might have shrunk up from starvation, but I'll tell you, my stomach was still there! If we'd had no food at all, the hunger pangs would have eventually gone away, but the Japanese gave us just enough food to keep hunger pangs alive so we would suffer!"

Sanitation remained a constant struggle as well.

"In the Philippines we had cold running water we could bathe in every day if we wanted to. In Japan, we bathed once a week, in a warm bath on Friday night. It was the only thing we could look forward to. The Japanese had a large wooden hot tub that fifteen to thirty people could use at one time. It was in a separate room and the Japanese used it every day. We could use it once a week, on Fridays, after they finished their daily bath. Of course, we bathed in their dirty water, but the water was still warm and it felt good."

Other sanitary needs went unfulfilled.

"We never had a toothbrush or any way to brush our teeth the entire time I was a POW. We had bad breath you could cut with a knife, but the prisoners didn't mind because everybody was in the same boat.

"We also didn't cut our hair; we all just let it grow. A lot of guys let their beards grow out as well though some of us had a razor with one blade to shave with. I think I was lucky enough to have two blades the whole time I was a POW so I could shave. Of course, I didn't have much to shave anyway."

The prisoners had also long acclimated to the idea of urinating and defecating with no means of cleaning themselves afterward. They found a new twist on their toiletry rituals in Japan, however, where the Japanese sold the prisoners' excrement to civilians as fertilizer.

"They would collect it and use it to fertilize their fields. The stench in the camp was horrible because of all the excrement. However, there is a funny side to this because someone sold the civilians on the idea that officers' excrement was worth more than anyone else's. So, the civilians paid more for excrement from the officers' toilet than for excrement from our toilet!"

As a result of their malnutrition and unsanitary conditions, prisoners continued to suffer from a wide range of diseases and continued to have next to nothing to combat them with. In addition to dysentery, prisoners had everything from large tropic ulcers and intestinal worms to jaundice, typhoid, tuberculosis and pneumonia besides the common jungle diseases of malaria, dengue fever, and the like.

Again, Larson proved luckier than most and suffered little physically during his year in Japan.

"Fortunately, I don't recall that our camp in Japan had any major illnesses, like appendicitis, and only twelve prisoners died that I know of when I was there. Some guys got pneumonia, but all of them survived it somehow.

"I did get an ear infection one time and the doctor said that all he could prescribe was hot packs. He told me he could arrange to get hot water from the mess hall. I put the hot water in a canteen and held it on my ear. It was so hot that my ear burned and blistered. The heat finally burst the eardrum. Boy, did that feel good when it happened. I didn't have to work while I had the ear infection. That was the only time I had a couple of days off during my captivity in Japan!

"I think our medical staff, who were prisoners just like us, spent most of their time frustrated because all

"As a prisoner you get to the point where you accepted your fate and made the most of where you were and what you had to work with. Deep down you always resented it, but you never dwelled on it. Self-pity could swallow up a man."

they had to treat us with was charcoal and hot packs because the Japanese kept any captured American medical supplies, as well as their own supplies, for themselves.

"Our doctors came up with a good stopgap method for diarrhea using the charcoal from burnt rice left in the bottom of the pans at the mess hall. After the cooks were finished, they would clean out the cauldrons and save the burnt rice. When prisoners got diarrhea, they were issued some burned rice to eat. It was basically charcoal and would help slow the condition."

The illnesses the doctors were trying to treat were rare and even unseen in a well-nourished society, reports Hampton Sides in his book *Ghost Soldiers*. As a result of malnutrition and unsanitary conditions, POWs of the Japanese "lost their voices, lost their hair. They lost eyes, they lost their hearing, they lost the signal of their peripheral nerves. Their teeth fell out. Their skin fell off. They developed a strange ringing in their ears. Rank metallic tastes soured the backs of their tongues. Their fingernails grew brittle and developed strange textured bands."

Six months before the war ended, the Camp Namachi prisoners received a package from the Red Cross (only the second Larson received during his entire captivity), which contained not only a can of Spam, the first substantial meat they'd had in years, but soluble coffee and some cigarettes.

"That Spam was heaven, and the coffee was a real

treat. Everybody knew I was a great coffee drinker but didn't smoke cigarettes. A lot of my friends who didn't drink coffee would trade their coffee for my cigarettes."

Aside from the Red Cross package and occasional earthquake, survival at Namachi was a daily grind. "You can use the word monotonous for 1944. We had no outside contacts. There was virtually nothing coming in and nothing going out. We just kept time out of our minds; we had to. As before, I lived from day to day and didn't worry about the past or tomorrow.

"People may find this hard to believe but as a prisoner you get to the point where you accepted your fate and made the most of where you were and what you had to work with. Deep down you always resented it, but you never dwelled on it. Self-pity could swallow up a man."

To survive the monotony, the prisoners would think up all kind of things to occupy their minds. Larson continued to focus on doing complicated math problems in his head, and like most prisoners, he thought about the food he would eat when he got back home.

"You'd be surprised at the menus people would dream up in their heads. People would project for one year what they would eat for every meal, every day. Even after we got home, food remained the focus and I'd often dream about what I would eat the next day."

Monotony ruled in Namachi at least until the end of 1944 when the prisoners began seeing American bombers flying over and hearing them drop their bombs on Japanese targets. In some cases the bombers unknowingly bombed prisoner camps and workstations, including the Yokohama shipyard where POW Dave Brenzel toiled. "If there was a cause of mixed emotions, the B-29 raids were it," Brenzel admits. "We never knew whether we were on target when those B-29s with their firebombs cruised over in insolent fleets. At times, we were in the center of a semicircle of fire when the all-clear sounded."

The bombing intensified throughout 1945, and American bombers started hitting targets closer to Larson's camp as well. "We could hear the bombs though we couldn't see the planes because bombing usually occurred at night and at a very high level.

"The B-29 bombers also mined an entire inlet close to our camp with magnetic mines. The Japanese had a large steel manufacturing plant there. Every once in a while, we would hear a 'boom' when a mine detonated. We didn't know whether a ship detonated one or it just detonated itself. But it was a good sound to hear. It was a real morale booster."

"One night, the steel plant in the town of Takaoka was firebombed. It was about fifteen miles from the POW camp. We knew bombing was happening because we knew what bombing was! Everyone left the barracks. The Japanese guards tried to run us back in but they couldn't. Then they left us alone. We even climbed on top of the roof. We could see the flames in the distance and hear the reverberations. We cheered. It was a real high point for us!"

As the bombings increased, the prisoners' morale rose and they began to believe they might actually see the end of the war and their American homes again soon.

"From the start, it was much different in Japan than in the Philippines because, in Japan, I think everybody felt deep down we were eventually going to get out of there. Once the bombing started, and we knew America was hitting the Japanese homeland, the feeling inten-sified a bit."

Though the promise of an actual future was more

tantalizing than ever, the hardened POWs also tried not to get their hopes up too high lest they fall victim to the kind of shattered hopes that had killed their POW friends back in the Philippines.

"We had lived this long, and we had indications that things were getting better, especially after a batch of British prisoners arrived from Singapore in early 1945. On their work details, the British prisoners would come back with smuggled newspapers, and some of their guys could read and speak Japanese so they would share some of the anecdotes with us, like how the Japanese were advancing to the prepared positions in the rear. The newspapers discussed a certain island, and then the next time it would be about this island, and then this island, etc. From this information, we could figure out the Americans were on the way! We knew that step-by-step the Americans were getting closer and closer, and we started thinking about home for the first time in a long time."

As the spring of 1945 turned to summer, the prisoners had more and more indications that the Allies were winning the war.

"When low-level bombing began at about 5,000 feet, we knew the end was pretty doggone close. When the first bombing started, we saw Japanese fighters taking off to intercept the American bombers but we never saw any Japanese fighters in the air after early 1945, so we knew the end was coming because the Americans were bombing Japan with virtually no air opposition."

The Japanese also had little in the way of antiaircraft defenses on the ground. "At night they had to rely on radar and theirs wasn't that accurate. Combine that with the fact that they didn't have very many fighters left, and you knew we were winning.

"Even when the bombs came close, we weren't

really scared or anxious. In fact, we would look forward to the bombing. When it started, everybody's spirits rose because we knew the end was coming. Especially toward the very end of the war, the bombing was around the clock and the Americans were firebombing heavily. We knew Americans wouldn't be able to bomb with such intensity if the Japanese defenses weren't all but gone. We knew darned well the end of the war was getting close!"

As the end of the war grew closer, the civilians became friendlier, Larson recalls, but the demeanor of the military guards did not change much.

Though the prisoners began to look forward to pending freedom, there were nagging rumors that the Japanese might execute them instead of freeing them. "We thought that might be a possibility but mostly kept such thoughts to ourselves. We did, however, all agree that if they lined us up to execute us one day we would revolt and charge them. But, we never spent time discussing it because either they would do it or they wouldn't and thinking about it wasn't going to change what might happen. You could really only survive if you thought just about that day and got through that day, not worrying about tomorrow."

"In fact, we learned after the war, that the Japanese did have orders to execute all prisoners if America invaded Japan. The original orders are now housed in the Truman Library in Independence, Missouri."

Still, in the end, being a prisoner of the Japanese proved far more deadly than fighting them. It's estimated that two out of five American prisoners perished in Japanese hands. And, according to Hampton Sides in his book *Ghost Soldiers*, the death rate in Japanese-run prison camps was twenty-seven percent, compared to four percent at prison camps in Germany and Italy.

Adding to the POW death count is the sad fact that more prisoners died at home in the years following their release from complications stemming from years of starvation and torture. Fewer than 1,000 American survivors of the Bataan Death March are alive today.

COMING HOME

On August 6, 1945, America dropped the first of two new weapons on Japan, atomic bombs that leveled the towns of Hiroshima and then Nagasaki (August 8). On September 2, 1945, the Japanese signed the formal unconditional surrender to America and her allies.

The thirty-some POW camps throughout Japan knew little of the surrender and nothing about the new weapons used to end the war. "I'm convinced that the atomic bomb shortened the war and saved all of our lives. I have since learned that the Japanese were also working on the bomb and knowing them as I did, I am sure they would have used it."

Though Larson and the other POWs had no idea how powerful a bomb had just exploded in Japan, by the beginning of August 1945, "we knew something was up because we hadn't worked for a couple of days," Larson notes. "Every morning, as part of our routine, we left the barracks and stood roll call while the Japanese made sure everyone was there. This day, after they called roll, we were dismissed. The guards stacked their rifles and took off. The only Japanese in camp after they left was the "One Armed Bandit" and the first sergeant. So, we figured the war had to be over. In fact, the surrender had taken place but we didn't know it."

American planes soon began to fly over the area of the camp, dropping notes to tell the POWs to mark their camps and stay put to await liberation.

"They wanted us to identify the camp with a big 'POW' on top of the compound so we would be rescued. So, we found some paint and a few ladders and climbed up and painted big 'POWs' on the building roofs. Once our location was identified, Air Force planes flew over every other day and dropped food and 'goodies' to us by parachute."

At other camps, some of these dropping containers ironically killed a few POWs who were over-eager about the food being sent. As prisoners rushed to one crate, another crate of food fell upon a hungry prisoner and killed him.

"Most items were dropped with parachutes. They even dropped big 55-gallon drums of soup, which had parachutes so they wouldn't burst when it hit the ground. One time, however, the parachute on a 55-gallon drum didn't open and it went right through the roof of a school by our camp and killed a Japanese student."

A few days after the guards left, the camp got a surprise visit from The Swedish Consulate from Tokyo.

"Our camp commander, Lieutenant Sense, called everyone together on the parade ground and the consulate told us the war was over and we were now living in an atomic age. Of course, we had no idea what the heck this atomic age he was talking about was. Surprisingly, everyone was quiet and subdued at the news that the war was over — maybe because we already knew it was when the Japanese guards stacked their rifles and left in early August. After that, the consulate left and we never saw him again."

For the first time in more than three years, Larson had a peaceful night's sleep. "I knew I had made it then! Fortunately, I was in fairly good physical shape compared to others in the camp, and I knew I would make

> "I will never forget the sight of the Golden Gate Bridge as we sailed under it. .... For some of us, like me, it had been six years since we'd seen that bridge, since we'd been home. And, I think they heard our roar of joy in New York City!"

it home. It was a peaceful feeling."

Soon after the consulate's visit in mid-August, a United States surveillance plane landed near the camp and the plane's pilot got out and talked to the POWs, telling them to stay put in the camp and that a rescue team would be by soon.

"He flew away, and nobody ever came to get us. Waiting to get rescued was especially nerve racking, knowing you're free but not being able to do anything about it but wait to be freed.

"There was no place to go; we just sat around the camp, talked about old times and, mostly, what we were going to eat when we got out. You would be surprised with the concoctions we cooked up in our heads!

"As long as we were in camp, food and essential items kept coming by airdrop. The planes would drop notes giving us a variety of information about what was going on. They even told us about the Women Army Corps (WACs) and the WAVES. We had no idea there were women in the service! They also told us about a point system and how you earned points. A soldier needed so many points to be discharged. Well, everyone that was a POW had more points than they knew what to do with! When we started totaling points, we thought we could sell some of our points to someone else!"

Meanwhile, the prisoners' food supplies from the Japanese increased and none too soon as most prisoners, like Larson, weighed 100 pounds or less. Some looked like they should have been dead.

"We received more rice, fish and soybeans from Japanese civilians who delivered our food daily by truck. American cooks prepared all the food we ate. One day the civilian guard who had been in charge of us at the machine shop came and invited the two of us from the shop to dinner at his house. Other than that, I never left camp."

By mid-September of 1945, more than a month after the surrender, the Namachi POWs were beginning to wonder if they would ever leave camp. No one it seemed was coming to rescue them.

"We stayed in camp until September 14 when our camp commander Lieutenant Sense finally went to the One-Armed Bandit and made it very clear that he expected a train at the siding the next morning. That day, everyone was issued new Japanese military uniforms, which we didn't mind because our clothing was pretty dingy. The next day, on September 15, 1945, a passenger train was there with good accommodations. The train even stopped to pick up box lunches, rice balls, apples, fruits, vegetables and other items. It was a feast to us!"

The One-Armed Bandit rode with the prisoners on the day-and-a-half journey and told the train master where to go, bringing the POWs to a hospital ship in the harbor. "The One-Armed Bandit helped us get to the hospital ship sooner than if we'd waited for a rescue. He had caused a lot of misery, but compared with other Japanese, he wasn't a bad guy. After the war Lieutenant Sense went back to Japan for the One-Armed Bandit's war crimes trial and testified on his behalf. As a result, he was exonerated and freed."

The Japanese commander's clout got the prisoners on the fast track to freedom, Larson says. "We had the right of way completely through! We went through Tokyo, which was all burned out and down to a bay where the hospital ship, Mercy, was waiting for us.

"When we boarded, everyone threw their Japanese clothes into the bay! That bay was loaded with Japanese military uniforms!"

The medical crew gave the POWs cursory physicals and sent them to bed for a day and a half. "After that, we could get up and walk around. We were getting three meals a day. We were headed for a rest and recuperation camp outside Manila, but the ship had to slow down and wait because they weren't ready to receive us in Manila."

The ship arrived amid the sunken war debris in Manila harbor four days later.

"I was surprised because we hadn't seen much of Manila the last time I was there when we boarded the Noto Maru. The Japanese had transported us in trucks from Clark Field to Manila and then directly to Bilibid prison. This time we were transported in open trucks and we could see how devastated everything was from bombing and shelling. It brought back some very unpleasant memories as well as some pleasant memories. However, everybody was euphoric when we sailed in.

"The Army had built this camp especially for military personnel's rest and recuperation, and we were anxious to get there. It was located about twenty miles south of Manila. After we arrived, the officer in charge said we couldn't leave. But, if we were hungry, we could go to any kitchen at any time and request whatever we wanted. If the cooks had it, they would fix it for us! They did, day or night!

"No one got sick that I know of, maybe because we'd been slowly eating more since the end of the war. Once I got there, I sure ate a lot of eggs and Spam and drank lots of milk!"

After two weeks of recuperating — during which time the air force recruiters pestered Larson about re-enlisting promising they'd fly him home "right now" if he did ("and I almost did!") — Larson and other POWs shipped to the one place they'd tried not to think of and could only think of for more than four years: Home.

The first stop was San Francisco, where Larson was put through a more intense physical and was hospitalized at Letterman General Hospital for two weeks.

"I will never forget the sight of the Golden Gate Bridge as we sailed under it. While my wife is the most beautiful thing I've ever seen, that bridge — as a symbol of America, of home — was the second prettiest thing I've ever seen. We were all so excited. For some of us, like me, it had been six years since we'd seen that bridge, since we'd been home. And, I think they heard our roar of joy in New York City!"

Larson also recuperated with food and fun. He was in good enough shape to venture downtown at night. Most servicemen on leave have one thing on their minds, and Larson was no different ... except his one thing was food, and plenty of it.

"One time a friend and I went to a restaurant. We got there about 7 p.m., and closed it down at 1 a.m. We just kept eating the whole time! We were always looking for something to eat. Food was always the prime topic! You would be surprised at the food concoctions prisoners had dreamed they would eat when they got home, and we tried to eat them all when we finally go there.

"Chocolate pie was one of the most popular foods we discussed having when we got home. In the Philippines, there was a weed, which we called pigweed. I don't know what its real name was. It was good when you cooked it. It was kind of oily so it went well with rice. Everybody said that when they got home, they were going to find some pigweed, cook it up, and eat it! People would plan out for a month what they were going to eat!"

Larson was soon back to his pre-war weight, though he was puffy with a lot of water retention from the rapid weight gain.

From San Francisco, Larson was transported by

Newlyweds Alf and Jane Larson in 1946.

train to Shick General Hospital in Clinton, Iowa, for three weeks where a special detail of military police came and escorted him to the Paymaster to receive back pay in cash.

"Mine was over six thousand dollars! Of course, the Internal Revenue Service wanted me to pay back taxes on all of that, but the government finally worked it out so no prisoners of war had to pay any back taxes."

After collecting his money, Larson's first priority was to see his parents. It had been nearly six years since he'd been in his Duluth home, and he went to great lengths to get out of the hospital on leave long enough to visit Duluth.

"It was mid-October 1945, and a soldier named Bob Boyer and I knew a fellow at the hospital who had bought a car. We all lived in Duluth so the three of us pitched in, bought gasoline, tires, and whatever the car needed. The hospital staff had also given us ration coupons, which were still being used, so we brought those home to our families.

"We drove to Duluth for our first weekend furlough, and I was dropped off in downtown Duluth, hopped on a streetcar and went straight home. My parents had no idea I was coming, though I had sent word that I had survived and then let them know I was in America as soon as I got to San Francisco.

"My parents didn't have a phone so I couldn't tell them I was coming. I just showed up on the doorstep and tried to open the screen door. It was locked so I knocked and waited. My mom came to the door. She looked at me and cried, 'Ohoooooooooooo!' I said, 'Here I am, mom!' It's funny she didn't faint.

"My mother tossed up her arms and said, 'You're home!' She came to me and we hugged and I started to cry. When my dad got home from work we repeated the scene all over again, and I cried again. It was a joyous reunion!"

Though they hadn't heard anything of their son's welfare for more than a year, Mrs. Larson never doubted that reunion would happen one day.

"My mother always believed I would come home. She never, not once, thought I was dead. I guess she had seen a newsreel and swore up and down that she saw me walking on the march. In fact, she went back to the theater several more times to make sure it was me. I don't know if it was or not, but she always believed I was still alive.

In all those years the only official word the Larsons had received from their son was a War Department telegram that he was missing in action.

"The War Department further asked my parents to claim the insurance policy the Army had on me that was a $10,000 life insurance. My mother refused because accepting the insurance money would have forced her to admit that I was dead, and she couldn't accept that."

That first weekend, Larson stayed in the home he'd longed to return to for so many years. "My room was up in the attic and I slept there that first night, in my own bed. So many memories washed through my mind."

Larson received two more passes to visit home from Clinton, Iowa. When he returned home he mostly stayed with his family.

"I really didn't want to have anything to do with anybody else. I just didn't. I needed to get readjusted to life after captivity and wanted to be left alone. We lived adjacent to the woods in the west end of Duluth in Norton Park. I spent lots of time in the woods before enlisting and during my first two furloughs home. I spent most of my time with the family or back in the woods wandering around my old haunts."

It wasn't until his third trip home that his parents convinced Larson to come with them for dinner at the home of old family friends, the Stenbergs.

"I tried every way in the world to get out of going, but finally my folks insisted I go, and I'm glad because I re-met the girl I soon married, their daughter Jane. I had known Jane when she was a little kid about 10 years old, and I was friends with her brother.

"Well, when I walked into the house, the first thing I saw was Jane stirring gravy. It was the woman of all the POWs' dreams. She was beautiful and she was cooking food! Here I was starved to death and food was always on my mind and I thought, "Boy! That's for me!'

"It was only later that I found out that her mother had just asked Jane to stir the gravy for her. Jane didn't really know how to cook then, but after I met her, even that didn't matter."

After returning to the Clinton hospital for a few more

Alf Larson kept this memory of his Air Force days after World War II, which he spent refueling planes like the one above.

weeks, Larson bought Jane a watch and sent it to her. He was soon pestering the hospital staff about getting discharged so he could rush back to the hometown girl of his dreams.

"I felt fine and wanted to go home. A young lady clerk was responsible for approving hospital discharges, and I happened to overhear her talking to another clerk about a certain type of perfume she really liked. It was for sale at the PX so I bought a bottle. Then, I attempted to bribe her so I could get on the discharge list. I went up to her and said I had something for her. If she would put me on the first shipping list, she could have it. When I showed her the perfume, she said 'okay.'

Larson was officially discharged from the Army Air Corps in March of 1946 at Camp McCoy, Wisconsin. He had received the Purple Heart, Military Combat Medal, Philippine Campaign Medal, Pacific Theater Medal and Good Conduct Medal.

The former POW had proposed to Jane within a month of their first meeting and they were married February 8, 1946, on Larson's mother's birthday.

As they adjusted to married life, Larson continued to adapt to life outside captivity. Physical reminders of his years as a POW still plagued the Minnesota native, especially his knees, which were damaged in the rock quarry accident in the Philippines.

"I had 10 percent disability because of my malaria and I couldn't run because of the knee injuries from the rocks I received at Clark Field. If I even walked too fast, I fell right down."

"Which is how I caught him," his wife of 56 years often jokes.

"When we met, I had no idea what to expect," Jane adds. "I hadn't seen him for a long time. When he didn't want to talk about any of what he went through, I didn't ask. I guess I figured if he didn't want to talk, I didn't want to listen. Other than bits here and there, he didn't talk about any of these experiences for years. I am hearing a lot now for the first time."

Both say Larson suffered few nightmares from his POW experiences, and he was largely able to tuck them away until Rick Peterson's interviews and this book project began. "I didn't really have nightmares about it until I started talking about it again. That brought back a lot of it."

The Larsons largely put the war aside, however, when they started their happy years together. Larson used his back pay to buy their first home in Louisiana, where the former POW worked for Dupont Corporation in Baton Rouge and began studying at Louisiana State University.

After he'd been in Baton Rogue for six months, Larson received a letter his sister had sent him during the war from her home in Sweden. "The Japanese had stockpiled all the prisoners' mail in Cebu and when the occupation forces came into Japan, they found and forwarded it. The letter eventually made it to me!"

In 1948, Larson, who had been serving in the Army Reserves since he returned from the war, finally took those recruiters up on their offer and reenlisted in the Army Air Corps and was soon a part of the newly formed United States Air Force. A technical sergeant, Larson was stationed with an air refueling wing in Tucson, Arizona. While there, he studied engineering part-time at the University of Arizona on the G.I Bill.

In 1950, the United States entered the police action in South Korea that Americans now call the Korean War, and the former POW was all too soon heading back toward familiar territory.

His air wing rotated to duty in Guam, a steamy island Americans had freed from Japanese control less than a decade before.

"Even when I was there with our air refueling squadron, there were still a few Japanese hiding out on the island that refused to surrender. Though they mostly stayed hidden, they would sometimes come out and kill someone. So, every time that we went to the swimming beach we did so with a contingent of Marines as guards."

During his service in Guam, Larson's refueling squadron rotated to six months' duty in Tachikawa, Japan — a station too close to bad memories for Larson's comfort. "I wasn't very thrilled to go back to Japan, that's for sure. I went to Tokyo one time on a pass just to see it, but that was it. I never left the base; I had no desire to see any more of Japan than I already had in World War II."

Larson's second war service was safer duty than his first. From air bases in Japan and Guam, the now master sergeant's squadron refueled B-50 bombers in the air for Korean missions. They were far enough behind the front lines and away from enemy aircraft that concerns of being shot down were nonexistent.

That didn't mean, however, that refueling was a safe job. "We used the British system of refueling at that time meaning the bomber would travel with a lone line with a grapple on the end and we'd lower a hose with a hook to it. Then, they'd reel our hose in and attach it. Getting hooked up like that was tricky because you had two pilots flying very close together and having to maneuver that close."

Larson says he was always aware that one small misstep could bring down both planes and their crews. "We lost a ship in California that way because the pilot got vertigo from flying so close. He thought he was flying straight but he wasn't. When he tilted the wing, both planes went down and their crews were killed."

In 1954, Larson was discharged from America's armed services for the last time. By then, the airman had logged more than 9,000 hours of flying time just since World War II.

He moved his growing family back to Baton Rouge where he was employed at Ethyl Corporation while continuing to study engineering at the University of Louisiana.

Though they'd suffered two miscarriages along the way, the Larsons were now enjoying three children, a son, Alf Larson Jr., and daughters Linda and Laura. Today, they have five grandchildren, one great grandchild and another great grandchild on the way.

In 1957, the Larsons returned to Minnesota and settled in Crystal, while Larson worked for Honeywell Corporation and continued his schooling at the Uni-

Alf Larson (center, back) stands with his future wife and their parents shortly after his return home from Japanese captivity.

versity of Minnesota. He eventually passed examinations by the Board of Registration and was licensed as an electrical consulting engineer through the state Registration Board of Electrical Engineering. He started his own business designing electrical specifications for commercial buildings.

After retirement in 1982, Larson began volunteering for the Minnesota Zoo. To date, he has donated more than seven thousand hours there. He also is a long-time volunteer at the Veterans Administration and an active participant in a local Prisoners Of War group.

As he reflects on all he endured as a soldier and POW to enjoy the life he once doubted he would ever live to see, Larson hopes Americans respect the sacrifices men like him made for their country.

"I was very fortunate throughout my war experience. I was transferred from the front lines, then was able to get out of Camp O'Donnell and somehow was sent to

Clark Field where conditions were better than in almost any other prison camp in the Philippines. Even on the Hell Ship I was fortunate to be close to the hatch, and my camp in Japan was not too bad when compared with the torturous experiences of other POWs there. They starved us and beat us but it wasn't past bearing most days.

"Still, like thousands of former prisoners of war and millions of servicemen, I did pay a price to serve my country. I especially hope that future generations will know the price that's been paid to get and keep their freedom. Sometimes that price is very high; sometimes ensuring freedom for others costs an American his or her own life, health and freedom. As a representative of the thousands of Americans who have paid a price for freedom, I can only hope that future Americans appreciate the sacrifices made by others to ensure our way of life."

EPILOGUE

By Rick Peterson

In April of 2000 I went to the Philippine Islands to visit the places where my friend Alf Larson had lived, suffered, toiled, and endured. I wanted to trace Alf's footsteps along the Bataan Death March path and in Camp O'Donnell, Clark Field, old Bilibid Prison, and Corregidor. And I wanted to see the new Veterans Federation Museum and the Manila American Cemetery and Memorial, erected in honor and memory of the thousands of veterans like Alf.

This old crossing marker is a silent reminder of the death train. Photo by Rick Peterson.

I contacted the Philippine Department of Tourism, and Marina Villanueva, Vernie Velardes-Morales, and other staff members assisted me in planning two trips.

That first trip in April 2000 traced Alf's footsteps during the Bataan Death March, accomplished by driving to and

Former POW Alf Larson and his friend Rick Peterson today. Photo copyright 2002 STAR TRIBUNE/Minneapolis-St. Paul.

following the entire Death March route. My second trip involved attending events commemorating the sixtieth anniversary of the fall of Bataan on April 9, 2002. The visits exceeded all my expectations due to the planning and escorting capabilities of my Philippines Department of Tourism field guide, Day Cruz, whose detailed itineraries and incredible knowledge of local history was so excellent that she was able to locate people who remembered the marches that went through their area. As a result, I obtained some great interviews, photographs, and valuable information that helped my quest to reconstruct Alf's experiences.

Today, the Death March route is well documented by kilometer markers and a variety of memorials. We began at "Kilometer 00" in Mariveles at the southern tip of the Bataan Peninsula. The park is located about four miles from where Alf was captured and began marching with his group of some 100 prisoners.

We drove about four miles north of the park and stopped. I got out of the car and took a short walk. In seconds, sweat was pouring off me due to the awful heat and humidity. I thought about Alf. It was 58 years to the day he was in this miserable place. And without any food or water! I shut my eyes, and tried to imagine all the brutality there. Many thoughts raced through my head, and I became appalled at the inhumanity of it all. It was truly a miracle *anyone* survived.

We continued north under a blistering sun so hot that our car's air conditioning could hardly function and the driver occasionally shut off the engine so it wouldn't overheat. We stopped to photograph each memorial along the way.

The major highlight of this trip was in San Fernando. With the help of local residents, we found the exact place where Alf Larson boarded the train to Capas. We walked by the old train station and followed visible sections of the original tracks. At times they were covered by either gravel or paved roads. An added bonus was the discovery of several unused, worn, and rusty railroad signs from those days. They looked very much out-of-place but stood like ghostly sentinels from the past, marking the original train route. The tracks, and roads covering them, led to the site of the former Capas Train Station. Here, prisoners who had survived the ride disembarked from the stifling boxcars and began the final march to Camp O'Donnell. Our journey ended by driving to the Camp O'Donnell memorials.

After touring Corregidor Island, the city of Manila, and old Bilibid prison, where Alf was housed for several weeks while he awaited transport to Japan, I returned home and revised my manuscript for the third time. Peg Meier, staff writer for the *Minneapolis Star-Tribune,* produced a fabulous, full-page article about Alf and his experiences as a prisoner of war. The article was published on Memorial Day weekend, May 2000, and I felt my task had been accomplished.

I didn't give much thought at first to attending the sixtieth anniversary of the Fall of Bataan on April 9, 2002. Then an e-mail arrived saying that the "Battling Bastards of Bataan" organization was organizing a "mini-march" from the Capas Train Station to Camp O'Donnell. Surviving veterans and families were going to participate. After a few months of checking, it appeared no one from Minnesota would be attending. I called Alf and asked him if I could represent him specifically, and Minnesota veterans in general, on the "mini-march." He gave his permission and members of the "Survivors of Bataan and Corregidor" gave theirs. I contacted Vernie Velarde-Morales, Philippine Department of Tourism, and arrangements were made. I was ecstatic when I learned Day Cruz would again be my guide! Then, news reporter Bill Sherck from KSTP TV in St. Paul, Minnesota contacted me about my trip. Both Alf and I were interviewed and the story ran at different times on Channel 5 news.

After spending twenty-four hours getting to Manila and three hours driving to Bataan, I was ready. With a sign around my neck reading, "Staff Sgt. Alf R. Larson," I nervously lined up with hundreds of march participants.

The march began at 6 a.m., and it was hot! My clothes were already soaked with sweat. The heat and humidity became oppressive as we walked.

I remember feeling anger at the Japanese soldiers for their inhumane and brutal treatment of the helpless, the wounded, and the sick. My anger was soon replaced with an overwhelming sense of pride for our veterans. Talking with veterans who had already made the walk in 1942 was an added blessing.

I walked the last mile of Alf's footsteps alone. I marveled at the strength and perseverance of the Americans and Filipinos who had walked that road. They didn't give up. The Japanese had captured their bodies but not their spirits!

It was a real privilege to represent Alf and other Minnesota veterans who couldn't walk those steps again. I stopped and looked at the countryside, exactly as it was that day sixty years ago. I turned around and looked backwards. The marchers were not far behind.

As I watched them, I proudly remembered what my son, Benjamin, told me before I left. He said that if God could give him one wish, he would go back in time, stand along the Death March road, and shake the hand of every prisoner who passed to thank them for their sacrifice.

Though I still wondered why God allowed somthing like the Death March to happen, I knew we didn't need to go back in time to shake the marchers' hands. God had been right there, in the midst of all the brutality and inhumanity, extending His hand and giving strength to His children.

When the rest of the group caught up to me, we finished the march at the site of the former Camp O'Donnell. It took about three hours to complete the walk.

For the next several days I attended more anniversary events. They were very patriotic and conveyed expressions of thanks to America from a grateful Philippine nation. I especially admired the camaraderie still displayed by American and Filipino veterans to one another through handshakes, smiles, and hugs.

Nothing else during the second trip impacted me as much as walking on that hallowed ground consecrated with blood.

We had water bottles and drank freely from them. When they were empty, we got another. Those men couldn't even get a drink from wells bubbling alongside the road. They were shot if they tried.

We were able to sleep in comfort. Those men couldn't and were forced to get up and march during the night after they had just settled in. Any rest time they had came in the form of standing for hours enduring an "Oriental Sun Treatment."

We could shower and clean up. Those men lived in their filth for days, weeks, and even years.

We had regular meals of our choosing. Those men were half-starved before the ordeal even began.

Added to everything else was the scourge of brutality. It defies my imagination, as I'm sure it did theirs.

Their only choice was to look straight ahead, put one food in front of the other, and live for the moment. It is a walk, a moment in time, that I shall never forget!

After my return from the second trip, the media offered some more pleasant surprises. Teri Kelsh, editor for Sun Newspapers, wrote another article summarizing this trip and the reasons for it. It was published in the forty-one metro area Sun Newspapers. Bill Sherck from KSTP TV produced another piece that incorporated some of the video I had taken during the "mini-march." It ran several times on Channel 5 local news. These blessings were more than I had ever hoped for and enabled me to share Alf's story of endurance and survival with so many others.

Kristin Gilpatrick's work in compiling my notes, filling in details of Alf's story, and the subsequent book born of our work ensures that generations of Americans yet to come can know of the valiant suffering and sacrifice that the men of Bataan endured for them and their freedom.

In many respects, the legacy of the Bataan Death March is the mystery of how one group of people could be so cruel to another. The original march is long over, but our love, respect, and honor for those who endured it continues. These patriots defended freedom, democracy, and the liberty of the American and Filipino people. The Death March has become a "march through time," and it will never be over. Out of eternal gratitude for those who walked that path, it must never end.

Bataan Death March memorials include (from upper left) the Fallen Soldiers Memorial, Mt. Samat Memorial Cross, and Camp O'Donnell's Filipino and Battling Bastards of Bataan memorials.

BIBLIOGRAPHY

Alf Larson Interviews. Kristin Gilpatrick. Crystal Lake, Minn. 2002.

Back to Bataan: A Survivor's Story. Unpublished manuscript of Alf Larson's World War II experience. Rick Peterson. Third Revision. Feburary 2001.

Battling Bastards of Bataan Web Site. http://home.pacbell.net/fbaldie/Battling_Bastards_of Bataan.html.

The Bataan Death March: A Collaborative Project and Web Site. Bataan Memorial Museum and New Mexico State Department of Education. http://www.sfps.k12.nm.us/academy/bataan.

The Bataan Project. Elizabeth Marie Himchak. University of San Diego, San Diego. 1999.

Captured on Corregidor: Diary of an American POW in World War II. John M. Wright Jr. McFarland & Co. Inc. Publishers. Jefferson, N.C. 1988.

Death March: The Survivors of Bataan. Donald Knox. Harcourt Brace Jovanovich Publishers. New York. 1981

Ghost Soldiers: The Forgotten Epic Story of World War II's Most Dramatic Mission. Hampton Sides. Doubleday. New York. 2002.

The Hero Next Door Returns: More Stories from Wisconsin's World War II Veterans. Kristin Gilpatrick. Badger Books Inc. Oregon, Wis. 2002

**The History of United States Naval Operations in
World War II: Rising Sun in the Pacific 1931-1942.**
Samuel Eliot Morison. Little, Brown & Co. Boston 1984.
The Janesville 99. Zarette R. Beard. Reel Produc-
tions' In the Hands of the Enemy Web Site. http://
www.explorationfilms.com/reelproductions/hands-en-
emy/report.htm.
My Hitch in Hell: The Bataan Death March. Lester
I. Tenney. Brassey's Inc. Washington D.C. 1995
**Prisoners of the Japanese: POWs of World War II
in the Pacific.** Gavan Daws. William Morrow & Co. Inc.
New York 1994.
**Some Survived: An Epic Account of Japanese Cap-
tivity During World War II.** Manny Lawton. Algonquin
Books of Chapel Hill. Chapel Hill, N.C. 1984.
**Surrender & Survival: The Experience of Ameri-
can POWs in the Pacific 1941-1945.** E.Bartlett Kerr.
William Morrow & Co. Inc. New York. 1985.
**Surviving Bataan & Beyond: Col. Irvin Alexander's
Odyssey as a Japanese POW.** Dominic J. Caraccilo.
Stackpole Books, Mechanicsburg, Pa. 1999.
**Unjust Enrichment: How Japan's Companies Built
Post-war Fortunes Using American POWs.** Linda Goetz
Holmes. Stackpole Books, Mechanicsburg, Pa. 2001.

Ben Steele was fighting with the 19th Bomb Group
at Clark Field before he joined the 7,500-plus Americans hiking the Bataan Death March. While a POW,
Steele sketched many drawings on scraps of paper and
with whatever drawing material he could find.

Though many sketches were lost when his Hell Ship
was sunk on its way to Japan, Steele recreated his
haunting images from memory, four of which are used
in this book. Most of Steele's drawings are in a Mon-
tana State University collection. Find out more about
them through the university's web site,
www.artmontana.com.

ACKNOWLEDGMENTS

by Rick Peterson

Obtaining Alf R. Larson's story was a challenge. Initially, he was reluctant to talk about his experiences, which had been "buried" in his mind for many years. For over a year, Alf and I engaged in "small talk," and I will never forget the day he agreed to "tell me his story." What followed were lengthy evening interviews, transcribing them from tape recordings, editing for accuracy, reinterviewing, and revising to complete the final manuscript. I am grateful he decided to relive his horrific World War II experiences so future generations may come to understand just how much past generations sacrificed for them. Thanks, Alf!

So many people became involved in my research and did so willingly and eagerly. In addition to Alf and all the hours he spent interviewing, editing, re-editing and proofreading, I would like to thank the following: Alf's wife, Jane; my wife, Ruth Peterson, who let my household chores and family duties slide without complaint during the years this project required; and my son, Benjamin Peterson, who participated in several interviews and asked questions which clarified specific events. I also am grateful for the music of Sandi Patty and Johann Sebastian Bach, which kept me awake at the computer during many late nights as well as for the efforts of Claire Ross and Harriet Lonergan who reviewed and proofread the initial draft of the research manuscript. In addition, thank you to: Claire Ross, Ivan Clements, Barbara Masters, and Kelly Luikart for providing a variety of technical assistance; Katherine Archer and Kinko's in Minnetonka, Minnesota, for graphic arts assistance and research manuscript printings; World War II Bataan historian Fred Baldassare for the use of his photographs and for reviewing the final manuscript for historical accuracy; former civilian Japanese prisoner of war, Sascha Jensen, for her timely encouragement, helpful suggestions on the manuscript format, and continuous support that proved so crucial to my completion of the work. Death March survivor and former prisoner of war Ben Steele for use of his illustrations. Marina Villanueva, Vernie Velardes-Morales, and staff from the Philippine Department of Tourism for financial assistance and planning for my two trips to Bataan.

Special thanks goes to Jake Carlson, Independent Web Developer and Day Cruz, Philippine Department of Tourism staff for their numerous contributions. Very special thanks to Bill von Bank, without whose assistance this book would not have been possible. And, my personal thanks is extended to anyone else that helped but is not mentioned here.

Finally we come to the soldiers of Bataan and Corregidor. I thank God for their tremendous and unselfish sacrifices. Each one has earned my eternal gratitude.

ABOUT THE
AUTHOR

Kristin Gilpatrick was born in Edgerton, Wisconsin, to educators Robert and Barbara Gilpatrick. A Cedarburg High School alumna, she graduated from the University of Wisconsin-Eau Claire in 1990 with a double major in journalism and Spanish, having studied a semester in Valladolid, Spain. In college, her lifelong passion for writing and history blossomed into a love for telling stories of the "everyday" people who made history.

She put that passion to paper as a reporter for newspapers in Illinois and Wisconsin, winning nine press association awards along the way. From 1997-2001, she was an editor for the Credit Union Executives Society, Madison, Wisconsin, and now works full time on her books.

For the past fiteen years, she has also been a big sister to two girls in Big Brothers/Big Sisters programs and is active in her church. She is married to Steve Halverson, an Edward Jones investment representative.

They live in Monona, where Gilpatrick is working on her third book in the *Hero Next Door*™ war history series, *The Hero Next Door*™ *of the Korean War*, due out in 2003. Gilpatrick is also the author of the recently released book, *Famous Wisconsin Film Stars*. Find out more about *The Hero Next Door* series and other Gilpatrick books at *www.badgerbooks.com* or *www.heronextdoor.org.*

We hope you enjoyed reading
***Footprints in Courage* and**
invite you to check out
these other World War II titles

• *Stalag Wisconsin* by Betty Cowley. Here is a compre-
hensive look at 38 Wisconsin prisoner-of-war camps
during World War II that held 20,000 Nazi and Japanese prisoners. ISBN 1-878569-83-X, $16.95.

• *The Hero Next Door* by Kristin Gilpatrick. Some
300,000 Wisconsin men and women served this country in World War II. Here are the stories of 14 of those
who played a small part in a massive war. ISBN 1-
878569-66-X, $14.95

• *The Hero Next Door Returns* by Kristin Gilpatrick. Here
are a dozen more dramatic stories from Wisconsin's
World War II veterans. ISBN 1-878569-76-7, $14.95

• *Destined to Live* by Kristin Gilpatrick. Luck of the Irish
saved Chicago area pilot Bill Scanlon from all of the
war's crashes and near misses. Or perhaps he was just
destined to live. ISBN 1-878569-79-1, $14.95.

• *Honor Bound* by D.A. Lande. This is the dramatic true
story of radio gunner Clarence Wieseckel's 250-mile
trek to freedom in Switzerland when his B-17 crashed
over Germany. $10.95

Ask for these titles at your local
bookstore, on the Web at
www.badgerbooks.com
or call (800) 928-2372